IAN BR

persuade YOUR customers TO PAY more

FROM NEW ZEALAND'S LEADING BUSINESS AUTHOR

Published in 2002 Brooks on Business

An imprint of Nahanni Publishing Limited
PO Box 34-179, Birkenhead,
Auckland 1309, New Zealand
Tel. (09) 419 0681 Fax (09) 419 0695
info@nahanni-publishing.com

Copyright Ian Royston Brooks 2002

ISBN 09583506 8 X

All rights reserved. No part of this publication may be reproduced, stored in a retrieval system or transmitted in any form or by any means, electronic, mechanical, photocopying, recording or otherwise, without the prior written permission of the author.

Design and Production by Aviso Design Limited
Printed by Graphic Resources Limited
Auckland, New Zealand

Contents

Introduction	"Why should I pay more?"	1
Chapter 1	Slashing the price? Think twice!	5
Chapter 2	Myths about pricing	19
Chapter 3	Facts about pricing	37
Chapter 4	Value is everything	55
Chapter 5	The zones of basic value	75
Chapter 6	The zones of higher value	95
Chapter 7	Persuading your customers to pay more	115
Chapter 8	Handling price objections	133
Chapter 9	How to profit from your relationships	147
Chapter 10	Your next steps	165
A final word		168
About the author		169
Other books by Ian Brooks		170

PERSUADE YOUR CUSTOMERS TO PAY MORE

The objective in business is to have profitable customers who stay with you for a very long time.

Introduction

"Why should I pay more?"

"Why should I pay more?" That is the question your customers are asking themselves every day. I suspect it is a question that has been asked since the time of the cavemen: "Why should I pay one mammoth tusk for those two spears?" In any case, it certainly is a question that is asked in today's market place. That is partly because the business environment in most countries is more competitive today, and partly because improvements in technology and productivity have reduced the cost of producing many products and services. It is also because we live in times of low or no inflation. But mostly it is because we have taught our customers to ask that question! The response of most companies to a competitive environment has been to drop their prices to win business. Most shoppers, for example, know that there is no point paying full retail for fast moving consumer goods because what they are looking for will be on sale somewhere - if not in this store then the next; if not today then next week.

Many companies are now beginning to realize the foolishness of doing business this way. If you reduce your prices, you are probably reducing your margins. If you reduce your margins, you will make less money - or maybe no money. You might even lose money. What is the point in doing that? The purpose of being in business is to earn a profit. Therefore the objective that should drive every business leader is to acquire profitable customers who will keep doing business with them for a very long period of time. The key word, of course, is profitable. Many companies have lost sight of that. I was talking to a newly appointed national sales manager the other day who told me he had just instructed his people to walk away from a deal that was losing the company money. It took someone who was new to the company, an outsider, to see the stupidity of chasing a deal that would lose money. His biggest challenge, however, was convincing his sales force that he had made a good decision! Of course, there can be strategic reasons for doing business at little or no profit. Perhaps you need to clear old stock. Maybe you want to attract customers with a loss leader. You might be prepared to lose money on the first job to demonstrate to a client that you should become their main supplier. But most companies are competing on price (and losing profits) for only one reason: they do not know how to compete any other way.

> Most companies are competing on price for only one reason:
>
> they do not know how to compete any other way.

Economists will tell you that money is simply the medium through which everyone competes for what they want. The art of making money, therefore, is to convince your customers to pay more for your products and services. And the trick to doing that, is to make your customers want what you have more than they want what your competitor has. Sounds simple? It is! Business may be tough but it is not complicated. When your customers ask why they should pay more, it is your job to have the answer.

Persuading your customers to pay more is tough to do in this market place where customers want everything for free yesterday. Nevertheless, increasing your prices is the best action you can take to improve the profitability of your business. Moreover, you can persuade your customers to pay more if you follow these four steps:

1. Do not compete on price.
2. Create superior value.
3. Price for profit.
4. Sell the value you have created.

This book will show you how to make these four key activities the main things for everyone in your business. This book will also help you to change what people think about. The focus has to be on customers not products or services. It has to be on retaining customers not finding

2

new ones. It has to be on maximising profit not on building market share. And, the focus has to be on achieving good profit margins not just on high sales.

Persuading your customers to pay more makes good business sense. It is also more rewarding in other ways. Most of us would agree with the American business executive who once said: "Selling only on price - where's the fun in that?"

Hey boss! I made another sale! Of course, I had to give them a big discount. But at least I made the sale. Isn't that great?

Chapter 1
Slashing the price? Think twice!

"The map of the economy is covered with more and larger patches of unprofitability... No-profit zones are the black holes of the business universe."
Adrian Slywotzky and David Morrison in The Profit Zone

Imagine if every time a football team got the ball, it kicked it downfield, back to the opposition. How successful would they be? I suspect, not very. Their opposition would quickly learn that was what they always did. They would be prepared for it, and they would take steps to counter it. To be effective, a sports team needs to have a variety of tricks to keep its competition off balance, and it is the same in business. So why is it that most business leaders reach into the hat and pull out the same competitive strategy every time? Reducing the price is a neat trick if used occasionally, but the magic quickly wears thin if the same rabbit appears every time. It also becomes very easy for competing magicians to better that trick and relegate the rabbit-pulling magician to the second division. Even the audience becomes jaded after a while. Ho hum. Another sale. Just another discounted product or service. As a result, you have to offer more to keep their interest. A 10% discount does not excite your customers any longer? I guess you will have to offer them 15% next time.

In a dog-eat-dog market place it is tempting to compete on price. Indeed, the practice of discounting to gain business is so widespread that I used to think most companies had forgotten how to compete on any basis other than price. However, I have realised that I was wrong. Now I think we never knew how to compete any other way. As you will remember, we used to do business in a regulated economy until the mid 1980s. In every major industry sector there was either one dominant

5

player, or just a few very established companies. Then the world changed. Deregulation paved the way for increased competition and all of a sudden we had to learn how to compete. Competing on price seemed the obvious thing to do, especially since in many cases prices were unnecessarily high, having been propped up for so many years by subsidies and the lack of competition. Lower prices meant smaller margins and that, in turn, meant that companies had to cut their costs. Although that was painful, especially to those people made redundant, it was relatively easy to do because, once again, subsidies and the lack of competition had encouraged inefficiency. Today, however, it is a different story. Most companies are as lean as they can be. Their employees know that every year they will be expected to do more and that the days of large annual pay rises have gone. Pressure is constantly brought to bear on suppliers to trim or even slash their prices.

Today the practice of discounting is so wide spread that whenever I buy something I always complain that the price is too high, even if I do not think it is, because nine times out of ten, vendors will respond by dropping their prices. For example, when I was building a house a few years ago, the painting contractors suddenly disappeared from the job saying they were not coming back. Now that left me in a real pickle because we were already behind schedule and I had to move out of the place I had been renting while the house was being built. I immediately telephoned several other painting contractors and explained my problem. One company, which came around that afternoon to look at the job, seemed really switched on. They told me they could start the next day and would put a gang of men on to make up some of the lost time. They seemed to know what they were doing and they had a good reputation. The estimator said he would fax me their quote later that same afternoon. I had already decided to use this company but waited for the quote to arrive before telling them. When it came, I saw their price was in line with their competitors' quotes, so I telephoned the estimator to discuss the job. "You say you can start tomorrow morning?" I asked. "And you'll put a gang of men on the job to move it along?" The estimator assured me they would. "And if you are not finished before we move in, you will be able to work around us?" I added.

"No problem," he said.

"Well, I'd really like you people to do the work, but your price is too high."

"Okay," he said. "I'll see what I can do."

An hour later he sent back a fax saying he would reduce the price by 10%!

Now what was the sense of doing that? Even if he had built an extra 10% into the quote, or even if the company was desperate for work, they did not have to give away that much of their profit (which, of course, is usually where the money to fund discounts comes from). The estimator should have said, "Excuse me sir, but didn't you say that you needed someone to start right away? And, didn't you want a gang of men to move the job along quickly? Then you said that you might need us to work around you and your family if you move in before we are finished? Well, we can do all of those things. And we won't walk off the job like the other crowd did! Also, we guarantee our work. So, sir, isn't that worth the price we quoted?" Of course, I would have said, yes. Wouldn't you?

If reducing the price is your weapon of choice, you should understand that it will be easy for your competitors to outclass you because all they have to do is pull a bigger discount out of their hat. Kmart, America's largest retailer ever to seek protection from bankruptcy, learned that lesson the hard way. In an attempt to bolster falling sales, they reduced their prices. Not surprisingly their major competitor, Wal-Mart, responded with even larger discounts. Of course, Wal-Mart, being the world's largest retailer, has deeper pockets. As a result, Kmart lost the price war, lost sales and may well lose their entire business.

Discounting destroys trust.

Ironically, these mini-price wars not only cost you money, they damage your relationships with your customers. Discounting destroys trust. First you said the product was worth $50 and then you said it was worth only $45. Now you are prepared to accept $40. Your customer begins to think that perhaps your offering is worth only $35, or perhaps even $30. Your customer begins to wonder what the true worth of your product or service is. They get tired of worrying about paying too much or wondering whether they would have got a better deal if they had gone elsewhere. And then there is always the nagging doubt that maybe you *do* only get what you pay for.

Returning to the football team, perhaps the worst part about always kicking the ball away is that they give up something of value every time they do. They lose possession of the ball and, although they gain field position in return, most of the time what they gain is less valuable than what they concede. After all, you cannot score points without the ball but it is possible to score starting from your end of the field. It is the same for business leaders who know how to compete only on price. They may gain increased sales or market share, but they give up margin and profit. Your pricing strategy, of course, should be related to your business goals. Do you want market share? Are you aiming to increase volume? Or, do you want to increase profit? They are not the same. Many business leaders have learned the hard way that market share or increased volume does not necessarily equal profitability. Whatever your immediate objective may be, never forget that the long-term goal in business is to have profitable customers who stay with you for a very long time.

Discounting has its place

Just as there is a place for kicking the ball downfield in football, there is a place in business for competing on price of course. But the effectiveness of price as a competitive weapon lies in it being part of a larger strategy, which is related to how the company wants to be positioned in the marketplace, how it wants to be seen by its customers and prospects. What do you want your customers to say about you? Do you want to be seen as the lowest priced supplier? That strategy can work, of course. Just look at retailers like Wal-Mart and The Warehouse, or airlines like Southwest Airlines and Ryanair. But these companies have reinvented their industries and organised their businesses differently from their competitors so that they have significant cost advantages. Consequently, their prices may be low but their margins are healthy. Discounting is a viable long-term strategy for such companies. This cannot be said of most businesses that slash

Are your prices too low?

The answer may well be yes.

Here's why.

Your company sells sunglasses for $10. The unit cost is $7. You're thinking about cutting the price by 50 cents. According to the best sales estimates, if you hold the price, you'll have a 100% chance of selling 1,000 units. If you cut the price to $9.50, you'll have an 80% chance of selling 1,250 units, and a 20% chance of selling only 1,000. What should you do?

Statistically speaking, options A and B are identical: Each produces a $3,000 profit. And since Option A is risk-free, it might seem like the logical choice. Yet when 60 managers responsible for pricing decisions were asked this question, most opted to reduce the price. When they were told that competitors were likely to match the cut, most still chose the cheaper price point. Even when they were informed that a new demand forecast showed that the cut would actually lead to lower profits, the majority still wanted to reduce the price.

This and many other studies indicate that pricing managers routinely set prices too low, sapping their companies' profits.

The Harvard Business Review

their prices, however. Usually their costs are as high as their competitors', or sometimes even higher. Therefore, discounting reduces or eliminates profits. Often it even results in losses. For these companies, there must be a strategic reason for discounting because it is not a viable strategy long-term. Just ask Kmart.

But even discounters have opportunities to persuade their customers to pay more. I recently purchased a ticket to fly between two cities in Australia. I bought it on the Internet from a discount airline (after all, a flight is a flight, and who needs a sandwich if the flight is only for an hour?). I was delighted with the price of A$135. But I also would have been delighted with A$142. This would have given the airline a 5% increase, which probably would have gone straight to the bottom line. The higher fare would still have been considerably cheaper than the competition's fare. So why is the discounter not charging more?

What do you want your customers to say about your company?

But discounting is dangerous

In my experience, most business leaders do not want their companies to be seen as the lowest priced supplier. It is not just that they cannot afford to be; they do not want to be. These companies want to position themselves as being the most innovative, the fastest, the most stylish or the most reliable. They want loyal customers who are impressed with the quality of their products and the level of their service. They do not want their customers to say they are the cheapest; they want them to say they are the best. Nevertheless, these companies slash their prices because discounting is their only competitive weapon.

Slashing prices now will make it impossible to hit profit numbers for this year – and in subsequent years – warn sales experts.

Sales & Marketing Management

They cannot imagine going into battle without it. They cannot conceive of another strategy working. The Generals leading the Allied Armies in the First World War felt the same way about the Cavalry. Unfortunately, the Germans had discovered tanks and machine guns. The carnage was great. The human suffering was unimaginable. Relying on discounting produces the same results in business. Just ask the managers at Kmart.

Unless you are one of those innovative companies who have reinvented their industry, lower prices nearly always equal lower profits, as First Electricity, a New Zealand energy retailer, discovered recently. About eighteen months ago, I was driving to town and in front of me was a city bus with a big advertisement for First Electricity on the back. It read: "All electricity is the same - ours just costs less." Can you imagine that? Here is a company spending its valuable marketing dollars telling customers and prospective customers that price is the only thing that matters. It is saying that customer service is unimportant, that billing accuracy counts for nothing, that continuity of supply is not an issue. All of this in a city which lived through months of blackouts in the CBD a few years ago! If I ran First Electricity, the advertisement would read: "Our electricity costs 10% more, but we guarantee that you will not run out!" Then a year ago, a headline in the Christchurch Press caught my

11

A lesson on the dangers of competing on price

The promise:

All electricity is the same - ours just costs less.

Advertisement by First Electric in 2000

The retreat

Firm admits prices were 'illogical'

"State-owned power retailer First Electric has admitted it has been selling electricity at 'silly' prices using tax-payers' money.

First Electric has abandoned its Christchurch customers on night and day tariffs, replacing the option of cheap night power with the standard day rate.

This week the State-owned enterprise blames a rise in the price of wholesale power for the decision."

The Press, Christchurch April 11, 2001

The defeat

Price rises a prelude to winter bill blues

"Bills for thousands of Aucklanders will go up by 11% or more from next month.

First Electric, which undercut competitors for most of the past two years says it cannot afford to keep losing money in Auckland. ….retail general manager, John Foote, apologised to customers for the big price rise."

The New Zealand Herald May 8, 2001

eye: "Firm Admits to Illogical Pricing." The first paragraph explained that First Electricity had admitted to selling electricity at "silly prices" and that Christchurch customers were going to have to pay more. One month later, I saw an article in the New Zealand Herald announcing that thousands of Aucklanders would be paying 11% more for their electricity this winter. The general manager of First Electricity, according to the article, explained that the company "could not afford to keep losing money in Auckland" and he apologised for the price rise.

It is not difficult to see why companies like First Electricity can get into so much trouble so quickly. Imagine that your company had sales of $1.5 million with total costs of $1.1 million, producing a profit of $400,000. Then imagine you discount your prices by 15% in order to gain a competitive advantage, or just to keep up with your competition. If sales and costs remain the same, what is the effect of this discounting on your profitability? Revue will drop 15%, of course, but since costs remain the same, profits decline to $175,000 - a drop of 56%. Try explaining that to the chairman of the board! Even if some of the costs are variable costs which will reduce with the reduction in sales, your profits are still likely to decrease by significantly more than the 15% discount. Nissan is a real-life example of this folly. The company has discounted its cars so heavily that it effectively stuffs US$1,000 in the boot of every car, according to industry experts. Toyota does not discount and its profit on similar cars is US$1000 higher.

Years of discounting and distress sales seriously undercut the value of the Nissan brand.

Fortune

But it gets worse. If you constantly tell your customers price, price, price, they will come to think that price is the only thing that matters, to the extent that you can undermine the brand you have worked so hard to build. Thus we have a very vicious circle. We talk to customers about the price because we expect they will focus on the price. They focus on the price because that is all we talk to them about. Today, you can expect that your customers will question the price. That does not, however, mean you have to cave in. It simply means that you must learn how to deal with the price objections (see Chapter 8). If you are in selling, this is your job. Ironically, some customers are moving beyond the issue of price faster than their suppliers. Last year I was meeting with some senior managers of a local authority who were complaining that they would like to see suppliers discuss the value they can add when they bid for work, but all the suppliers want to talk about is price!

> "The long-term profitability of European airlines is under serious threat."
>
> Chris Avery, airline analyst for J.P. Morgan & Chase.

The more we give in to price pressure and the longer we offer discounts, the deeper the hole we dig for ourselves. Constant discounting within an industry simply has the effect of training shoppers to wait for sales. The motto of many shoppers is "Never pay full retail." If what you want is not on sale somewhere today, just wait a week or so. Some store is bound to be having a sale. I guarantee that this weekend most appliance stores in your area will have items on sale. Constant discounting also undermines your brand. It tells a customer that attributes such as quality, exclusivity and luxury are not important. Just price. Discounting can threaten not only your profitability, but that of your entire industry. Established airlines in Europe are under serious attack from discount airlines such as Go and Ryanair. At the moment, the discounters are doing very well but there may be storm clouds on the horizon. "The long-term profitability of European airlines is under serious threat," says Chris Avery, an airline analyst for J.P. Morgan & Chase.

Profit is not a natural condition

Bill Gates once said, "Profit is not a natural condition. It takes some special work to create." Part of that special work is being able to price for profitability. One of the best ways to increase your profit is to manage price effectively, yet this is one activity managers often shy away from because they are afraid that if they increase their prices they will alienate their customers, lose sales and see their market share dwindle. Instead, they feel more comfortable managing costs or increasing sales. But these are not easy to do. Most companies have ripped as much cost out of their business as they can and in a crowded and competitive market, increasing sales is difficult, time consuming

and expensive. Increases in price, on the other hand, are much more effective in enhancing profitability. In fact, a price increase can have an effect on profitability which is 3-4 times greater than that coming from a proportionate increase in sales. One producer of consumer durable products increased its operating profits by nearly 30% with as little as a 2.5% improvement in its price. Similarly, a manufacturer of industrial equipment boosted operating profits by 35% with only a 3% increase in price. A study in the United States by McKinsey suggests these results are typical. In fact, just recently I was working with a company in Great Britain, which although it operated nation-wide, was only the fourth largest company in its industry. Last year, this company, which operates in a very cut-throat marketplace, increased its

Many otherwise tough-minded managers shy away from initiatives to improve price for fear that they will alienate or lose customers.

Harvard Business Review

revenue by many millions of pounds over the previous year, and 83% of that increase came because they persuaded their customers to pay more! Without realising it, many managers are walking away from significant amounts of money, all because they do not dare set higher prices.

When your customers buy only on price, they are saying that your product and service is no different from that of your competitor's in their eyes. That means one of two things. Either you have not created any extra value or you have not communicated the extra value you have created. Both of these activities are part of your job. They are the special work you have to do if you want to earn a profit.

Price is not *the* most important issue to consumers. What matters most is whether the seller has a product or service that customers value. Price becomes the issue only when customers cannot see the difference in value between two offerings. In other words, when they perceive the product or service to be a commodity item. Unfortunately, most products and services, today, are commodity items in the eyes of the customer because the quality differences between products (and even customer service) in similar markets is very small. As we will see in Chapter 5, you can change that by surrounding your basic offerings with add-ons that the customer values. The focus will not then be on the price.

> *The right price can boost profit faster than increasing volume will; the wrong price can shrink it just as quickly.*
>
> Harvard Business Review

Persuading your customers to pay more makes good business sense since research suggests that even a 1% increase in price will make a significant difference to your bottom line. If you are not convinced that slashing prices is bad for business, if you continue to yield to the pressure to discount, the fate of the margin destroyer will be yours.

An average increase in price of 1% would boost net income at:

Fuji Photo by 6.4%
Nestle by 16.7%
Ford by 26 %
Philips by 28.7%

And your company?

Power Pricing *by Robert Dolan & Herman Simon.*
Published by The Free Press, New York, 1991.

Summary

- Most businesses compete on price and price alone.
- Discounting has its place, especially if you re-invent your industry.
- But it is a dangerous strategy because it destroys trust, goodwill and profitability.
- Pricing for profitability is critical to business success.
- There are alternatives to discounting because price is not the issue.
- Customers want good value, not lower prices.
- Most of us do not understand what our customers value.
- Avoiding discounting, or even raising prices by as much as 1% will have a marked positive effect on your bottom line.

Think about it

List all the occasions in the last three months when you competed on price.

What did it cost you to do that?

What will happen if you keep doing that long-term?

If you were one of your competitors, how would you respond ?

Chapter 2
Myths about pricing

People buy for emotional reasons, not logical ones.

There is probably no topic in business that is more shrouded in myths than pricing. This is unfortunate because, as we have seen, there is nothing that can have a greater impact on profitability than pricing. Therefore it is worth challenging these myths because clinging to them with blind faith could threaten your business.

Myth 1: Price is THE issue

Perhaps one of the biggest myths in business today is that price is what matters most to the consumer. This is simply not true. A recent survey by Grey Advertising in Canada, for example, found that only 37% of those surveyed said they compared prices, down from 54% in 1991. An Australian study discovered that people look at use-by dates and country of origin, more than price. Woolworths is one of the most profitable grocery stores in Australia but it is certainly not the cheapest. Another study, this time looking at Internet use, found only 19% of net shoppers used the net to compare prices. One of my clients recently surveyed their customers and found that although they are in a very competitive market, price was listed third, behind convenience and quality, in the list of factors affecting their customers' decision to purchase. Price is not even the major issue for people buying online. Amazon.com, for example, is more expensive than many of its competitors.

A Canadian survey found that only 37% of people compared prices.

But you do not need to look at the research evidence to know that other factors influence the buying decision more than price. You just have to look at your own behaviour. Can you put your hand on your heart and say that you always (or even usually) buy the lowest priced product? In fact, do you really compare prices every time you buy

19

something? Do you occasionally shop at convenience stores where convenience costs more? How far would you drive to save 2c per litre on petrol? When you shop at a 'discount' store, do you know for sure that the prices you are paying are actually cheaper than you could get elsewhere? And, how does the idea of being operated on by a budget brain surgeon strike you! The truth of the matter is that people buy for emotional reasons, not logical ones. Indeed, approximately 70% of the buying decision is made for emotional reasons.

Nearly all of us frequently and knowingly pay more if there is something else being offered such as convenience or reliability. A good example of this is colour televisions. When they first came out in the 1970s, price was the main issue. A number of companies produced similar products and customers made their choice based on

the price. Quality was never an issue because one manufacturer's product was as good, or as bad, as another. Then the Japanese entered the market and the game changed. The Japanese sets were of a higher quality and, although they were more expensive, they were still within people's range. The Japanese won the business. Quality was the main issue for consumers and they were prepared to pay a premium for it.

The power of a brand is a much more important issue than price, especially at a time when consumers are overwhelmed with choices. As I've said before, money is simply the medium by which everybody competes for what they want, and the more you want something, the more you will pay for it. Money is emotion made tangible - a channel into which all desires are poured. The purpose of a brand is to stimulate those emotions. The brand owner has decided how they want you to feel when you think of their brand, when you see their logo and when you use their product or service. Brand leaders are seldom the cheapest and examples of the cheapest brand having the largest market share are rare. Moreover, powerful brands have customers who are more committed to the brand and are therefore more likely to repurchase.

Certainly, price is *an* issue. Most consumers will try a competing product if the price difference is big enough *and the risk of doing so is not too great*. They will even switch to a competing brand if the price difference is big enough. Your price has to be within the capability of your target market and, unless you have something that makes your product very special, your price has to be within sight of your competitor's, probably no more than 15% to 20% higher. Admittedly, there is evidence to suggest that consumers in New Zealand are more price-sensitive than Australians.

Research by Westfield's, the operators of large shopping malls in both countries, has shown that New Zealand consumers are very focused on price while Australians are more concerned about receiving value. But I wonder if New Zealand shoppers push for lower prices because, as we saw with First Electric, we have been teaching them to believe that price is the most important issue? Even in New Zealand, however, you do not have to be the lowest price supplier. Price is an issue for consumers, but it is not *the* issue.

Is price really THE issue for you?

Do you always (or even usually) buy the lowest priced product?

Do you really compare prices every time you buy something?

Do you occasionally shop at convenience stores - where convenience costs more?

How far would you drive to save 2c per litre on petrol?

Would you buy a $6000 used car that might need repair work in the near future or an $8000 car that probably will not?

Do you know the prices of most things you buy at the grocery store?

When you shop at a 'discount' store, do you know for sure that the prices you are paying are actually cheaper than you could get elsewhere?

Would you like to be operated on by a budget brain surgeon?

Do you look for what is on special before you buy your usual brand?

Have you ever been put off because the price was too cheap?

Do you ever treat yourself?

Do you ever think, "You can't go wrong buying quality"?

Then why would your customers think and behave any differently?

Many of you, of course, will be selling business to business and have to deal with purchasing managers who have only one objective and that is to beat down your price. There is no doubt that price is a major issue in this world, especially in industries such as construction where the tender process is widely used. But again, price is not *the* issue. For nearly 15 years I have organised seminars for companies where two or three of their customers come and talk to the entire staff about what they require from their company. Nearly every customer has the same message. "Price is important," they say, "but reliability is more important." These customers know that if their suppliers let them down, then they will end up letting their customers down, and that could have serious financial consequences for them. Of course, purchasing managers will not talk about this when they are trying to persuade you to slash your price. Perhaps you should?

If price is THE issue...

Why are sales in full service restaurants increasing at the rate of 6% per year?

Why have registrations of large motorcycles such as Harley Davidson increased 150% in the last decade?

Why are we not all driving Ladas?

The consequences of making a poor purchasing decision are much greater for a company than for an individual. An individual may have wasted a few hundred dollars and suffered some inconvenience or disappointment. But a poor purchase by a company may cost it a few hundred thousand dollars and some very valuable customers. So why are purchasing managers focused on price? Because their job encourages them to look only at the cost side of the equation, not on the benefits. They work on the assumption (as their boss does probably), that if they can reduce their costs, they can increase their profits. On the face of it, there is some logic to this. But, as I have said, if a cheaper price results in increased operating costs and lost customers, where is the saving? Moreover, paying more for a higher quality product or service might help the company to charge more to its customers. As we will discuss later, if your product or service contains increased value, then it will increase the value of your business customer's product or service. Your customer should be able to translate that into higher prices for them. That was the strategy behind the "Intel inside" campaign.

> ## Value not price online
>
> Online business buyers usually value brand and service over price. Two new studies challenge the conventional wisdom that business-to-business (B2B) buyers use the Internet almost exclusively to hunt for bargains.
>
> Each shows online B2B buyers value strong brands and quality of service ahead of price.
>
> It's a mistake to sell online at bargain prices while slashing personalised service to cut costs. Instead, use the Internet to reinforce your brand distinctions and improve customer service while maintaining prices.
>
> *The Main Report*

Another reason why managers and business owners resist their supplier's price increases is that they do not know how to on-sell the increased price to their customers. I am always amazed when I see commission salespeople complain about a price increase. You would think that if you were being paid a 20% commission and the price of the product increased from $500 to $600 you would be happy. After all, that would mean that you would earn an extra $20 for every sale.

But most salespeople do not think that way. The thought that comes into their minds is that a price increase will make it harder to close the sale. If you are a professional salesperson however, this problem is not a threat but an opportunity. The trouble is that most small businesspeople are not sales people. They are good plumbers, doctors, inventors or shopkeepers, but selling is not what they enjoy. That means they find it difficult to compete on any basis other than price, and therefore they resist any price increase from their supplier. The supplier's best strategy in this situation is to teach their customers how to sell. Some companies, like PPG Industries in New Zealand are doing this with extremely positive results.

Myth 2: The market sets the price

In this customer-centric world, another pricing myth is that the market sets the price. This myth says that customers will tell suppliers what they can charge and that the vendor is powerless to do anything about it because, according to Myth 1, price is the issue. To believe in this myth is to believe that marketing has no effective role to play in business success, that brand is unimportant and that sales people are simply order-takers. Perhaps your marketing is ineffective. Perhaps you do not have a very powerful brand. Perhaps your salespeople are order-takers, but it does not have to be that way.

You do not have to be passive and accept what the market chooses to offer you for your wares. You can actively influence the amount your customers will happily pay. First, as we will discuss in Chapter 4, you can create a demand by finding those problems that bother your customers

Lowering rates at the whims of customers or the economy can severely damage an organisation.

Sales & Marketing Management

so much that they will be glad to pay your price to have them solved. It is not enough just to identify the problems, however. You need to understand what those problems are costing your customers and what it would be worth to them to have them solved. Secondly, you must discover what would enhance the value of your product even more.

What do your customers value? Convenience? Speed? Reliability? Personal service? Luxury? Expertise? You then wrap these value enhancers around your basic offering. Finally you must sell the value you have created (see Chapter 7). Through attractive packaging, creative advertising, and skilled selling you can show your customers the value your offering can provide them.

If it is that simple, why do people fall into the trap of believing they must accept what their customers offer? I think it is because our mindset is wrong. As I said in Chapter 1, the main reason we do not put our prices up is because we are afraid. Thus when someone tells us that the customer is prepared to pay only $65 we say to ourselves, "If they tell us they will pay only $65, we could never get them to pay $75." But that kind of thinking just closes the mind. What we should be asking ourselves is: "What would we have to do to get our customers to pay $75?". That is 'can-do' thinking and it opens the mind to endless possibilities. If you cannot think of anything, remember that you could always attach a $50 to your product. Then your customers would certainly pay $75 for it! So, what else could you do? There is always something. You just have to discover it.

What would you have to do to get your customers to pay the price you would like to charge?

This myth that the price is set by the market also implies that customers know what they are prepared to pay. They do not, and there was a great example of this in New Zealand a few years ago. An overseas company planned to introduce a new ice-cream product that was essentially an ice-cream on a stick. Admittedly, it was a very tasty and upmarket ice-cream on a stick. When their New Zealander competitor got wind of this, they did some market research by putting focus groups together and letting them taste the new product. Among other things, the New Zealand company asked people in the focus groups whether they would be prepared to spend $2, which was the asking price, to buy the product. Overwhelmingly, they said, no. This came as a great relief to the company and they decided that the $2 price would remove any threat the product might have posed, and they decided to ignore it. I guess the Australian company forgot to do any market research because they launched the product in New Zealand just as they had planned to do. It took off. Within a few months this 'outrageously priced' ice-cream on a stick had captured 33% of the novelty ice-cream market!

Successful business people do not let the market or the competition set the price. They understand that price is a key part of the profit equation and therefore they are not prepared to give up control of their price to someone else. They believe that by understanding their customers, designing and packaging the right offering and by selling the value they have created, they can manage price just like they manage any other profit driver.

Successful business people do not let the market or the competition set the price.

Myth 3: You must match your competitor's price

This myth is the result of believing the first and second myths. It says that since price is *the* issue and is set by the market, you must match your competitor's price because if you allow them to undercut you, then you will lose sales. In reality, the only time you have to match your competitor's price is when there is absolutely no difference between your competitor and you. No difference in your offering, your company, your brand, your marketing or your ability to sell.

Price is *the* issue only when customers perceive the offering to be a commodity item available from a number of companies who are just as good, or as bad, as each other. Banks have this problem. For most customers, a cheque account is just a cheque account and a mortgage is just a mortgage. What is worse is that according to research, most of us dislike our banks but do not switch to a competitor because we believe that they would be no better. Better the devil you know! In this situation, new customers are likely to make their buying decision based on price. Banks have realised that for several years and therefore have sharpened their pencils to get new business. As a result margins on loans have dropped significantly as any banker can tell you, and to make up for this, banks introduced user-pay fees. The trouble is, most of us hate the fees and this just reinforces our view that one bank is just as greedy as another and so we may as well chose the one with the lowest price. A couple of years ago, banks realised the folly of their strategy and are now working very hard trying to differentiate themselves and their products from their competitors. Most are finding

Take a lesson from Starbucks

Look at how Starbucks transformed a functional product into an emotional one. In the late 1980s, General Foods, Nestle, and Proctor & Gamble dominated the U.S. coffee market. Consumers drank coffee as part of a daily routine. Coffee was considered a commodity industry, marked by heavy price-cutting and an on-going battle for market share. The industry had taught customers to shop based on price, discount coupons, and brand names that are expensive for companies to build. The result was paper-thin profit margins and low growth.

Instead of viewing coffee as a functional product, Starbucks set out to make coffee an emotional experience, what customers often refer to as a "caffeine-induced oasis." The big three sold a commodity – coffee by the can; Starbucks sold a retailing concept – the coffee bar. The coffee bars offered a chic gathering place, status, relaxation, conversation, and creative coffee drinks. Starbucks turned coffee into an emotional experience and ordinary people into connoisseurs for whom the steep $3 per cup price seemed reasonable. With almost no advertising, Starbucks became a national brand with margins roughly five times the industry average.

The Harvard Business Review

it to be an uphill battle but some, such as ASB Bank, BNZ and WestpacTrust, are winning by improving the way they look after their existing customers. As a result, they do not have to have the lowest prices in the market.

You can avoid finding yourself in this predicament by differentiating your offering, building a distinctive brand, learning how to sell the value you have created and by mastering the handling of price objections. None of this is easy to do, of course, but then trying to make a profit while following a competitor bent on destroying the margins in the business is not easy to do either. If you do not think so, ask grocers, banks, insurance companies, airlines, retailers, travel agents, oil companies and manufacturers. Any fool can draw a line through a number and write a smaller number underneath, and many do! Persuading your customers to pay more is a lot more challenging but it is a lot more rewarding since you are likely to stay in business longer. The issue is not how your customers perceive the price of your offering compared to the price of your competitor's, but how they perceive the *value* of your offering compared to that of competing products and services. In fact, price is often the enemy of differentiation. If you find yourself having to match your competitor's price to get the business, you know that you have failed to differentiate yourself from your competitors. In the eyes of your customer, you are just another company supplying a commodity product. You should be directing your attention to remedying this root cause problem, not addressing the symptoms by lowering your prices.

Any fool can draw a line through a number and write a smaller number underneath. And many do!

Myth 4: You have to lower your prices to attract business.

If you believe the first three myths, you are likely to believe this one, too.

This myth does not just say that lower prices increase demand, which may have some truth to it (see Chapter 3), but that you *must* lower your prices if you want to increase sales. This is simply not true. If it was true then BMW cars, Rolex watches, Business Class travel and rare antiques would not attract many customers. Indeed, several companies have discovered that raising prices can increase sales. When online retailing became established, nearly everyone expected prices to be driven downwards. Recent research into online retailing in the book business in America has shown this has not happened. Moreover, the studies reveal that many online booksellers have discovered they can increase their prices and increase their sales. I have seen this happen in New Zealand, too. The chief executive of a major insurance company told me recently his company increased the price of one of its products, making it the most expensive in the market place, and saw sales increase as a result. On the other hand, there are many examples where lower prices do not stimulate sales. Skoda and Lada are good examples of this.

A corollary of this myth says that if you are second into the market with a new product then you must undercut your competitor in order to steal business from them. The drug manufacturer Glaxo proved this is not the case when they launched their ulcer medication, Zantec, after their competitor had introduced Tagamet. According to conventional thinking, Glaxo should have priced Zantec 10 percent lower than Tagamet but Glaxo's senior managers believed that Zantec was a better product. Their drug had fewer side effects, it interacted less with other drugs a patient might be taking and it had more convenient dosing. Glaxo believed that not only had they created more value, but that they would be able to sell the extra value to the market. Accordingly, they set the price for Zantec higher than the price of their competitor's product. In spite of the higher price, Zantec became the market leader. Glaxo then increased the price further and sales continued to expand.

Within three years of its launch in 1989, the Lexus accounted for 2% of Toyota's unit volume and nearly one-third of its operating profit.

Myth 5: You CAN win a price war

The only thing worse than discounting is getting into a price war. Price wars are the business equivalent of playing chicken, as in James Dean's movie *Rebel Without a Cause*, where two drivers head towards each other at breakneck speed. The winner is the one who does not swerve away (assuming he lives), and the one who swerves is branded 'chicken'. If both stay the course, the result is disaster.

As in all wars, ultimately everyone is the loser in a price war. Customers may initially gain some short-term benefit until one or more of the combatants falls over. Then as the victor increases prices to recoup its losses, customers discover they are no better off than they were before war was declared. Often, they are worse off. As soon as Ansett collapsed in Australia in 2001, Qantas increased its prices on those routes where it no longer had a competitor.

It is very difficult to win a price war. This is because all your competitor needs is access to a pencil so they can mark down their prices even more than you did. Dropping prices is a bottomless well! As Michael Porter says, slashing prices is insanity if your competitors can go as low as you can.

> *What's the surest way to kill revenue, profit and customer loyalty? Get into a price war.*
> Canadian Business

Even if you do succeed in maintaining the lowest price, there is the problem of how to remain profitable. Zellers, a large chain of department stores in Canada repositioned itself a few years ago as having the lowest prices. Its slogan was: "Where the lowest price is the law." That was a bold move in a market where Wal-Mart was a major player! I don't know whether they succeeded in having the lowest prices but I do know that they replaced the CEO and developed a new strategy just in time to avoid bankruptcy.

There is also some evidence to suggest that price wars are becoming ineffective in stimulating sales. According to an article in *BusinessWeek* (July 30, 2001) "the combination of a sluggish economy, mature markets and more efficient products has taken the poop out of price wars." Price wars, the article maintains, are only marginally boosting sales these days while they are completely eroding earnings. And the problem is that prices and margins hardly ever bounce back! Compaq, for example, lopped 50% off its PC prices in 1992, and although that stimulated sales, its margins fell from 37% to 24% and have rarely been higher than 27.4% since. Consequently, although sales doubled from 1990 to 1993, pre-tax profits fell from $641 million in 1990 (based on sales of $3.6 billion) to $616 million in 1993 (based on sales of $7.2 billion). Overall, sales doubled and profits dropped. Not a good result.

> *"It used to be that you could cut prices and people would buy more. Now there aren't customers for this stuff at any price."*
>
> Martin Reynolds, an analyst in the computer industry.

There is just no getting away from it. Price wars are destructive and unprofitable - not just for your business, but perhaps for your entire industry. Look at the airline wars of 1992 where the major American carriers went toe to toe in a vicious price war. The result was record numbers of passengers travelling – and record losses! According to the *Harvard Business Review* (March 2000) some experts estimated that the amount of money lost by those airlines in that one year was greater than the combined profits for the entire airline industry from the time of the first commercial air flight until 1992.

Myth 6: Discounters are successful because they have lower prices.

There are two types of retail stores that are succeeding in today's marketplace: low-cost stores and up-market retailers. It is the stores in the middle that are failing because they are neither one thing nor the other. So yes, discounters are doing well even though they charge lower prices but there is more to their success than simply lower prices.

Discount retailers such as The Warehouse, and low cost suppliers such as Virgin Blue, may have slashed their prices but they have not slashed their margins. They have been able to protect their profits because of the way they have structured their businesses. Their cost structure is typically significantly lower than that of their competitors because of the way they buy, the level of service they provide or the range and type of products they stock. As a result, a competitor with a more traditional cost structure who tries to match them on the basis of price is usually in for a rough ride – as anyone who has challenged Southwest Airlines knows.

Even for low-cost retailers, the question is what would they gain if they increased their prices by a few percent? This has occurred to them, I assure you, and many of these retailers are very good managers of price variation. Wal-Mart, for example (on which New Zealand's Warehouse is modelled), is a low-cost retailer. It is also the largest retailer in the world and one of the top five companies in the Fortune 500. Wal-Mart is reputed to be the best manager of price variation in the business. This means they charge low prices on those items customers expect to be cheaply priced and higher prices on those other items where customers are less price sensitive. This is simply the loss-leader concept applied in a more sophisticated way and on a wider scale but it is extremely effective.

Many successful discounters know that it is the perception of a bargain that matters, not the reality. I know of one chain in Australia which rents vacant stores in malls on a temporary basis, sticks up hand-lettered signs announcing bargain merchandise, sticks high prices on the merchandise, and watches the customers flock in and the goods flow out.

Can you afford to believe these myths?

You cannot afford to believe these myths and make price the issue. Even in tough economic times, the costs of doing business are creeping upwards, and some are leaping up. Take the costs of sales, for example. Research from the United States indicates that the average cost of a sales call has jumped 5% in the past year. It is even worse for companies that focus on creating value and providing solutions. They spend twice as much on sales calls as those companies who focus simply on the transaction.. These costs have to be covered and margins have to be protected. As I keep saying, the objective in business is to have profitable customers who stay with you for a long period of time. The key word is *profitable*.

Are you missing out on profits, or worse, heading for disaster, because you are letting one or more of these myths influence your approach to pricing? What is it costing you to hold on to these beliefs?

Summary

- Price is NOT the issue. People buy for emotional reasons more than logical ones. Research shows that even for business customers price is not the main issue.

- The market does not set price. You do not have to be a passive price-taker. There are things you can do to persuade your customers to pay more.

- You do not have to undercut or even match your competitor's price. The market leader is usually not the lowest priced. What you do have to do is differentiate your offering.

- You do not have to lower your prices to attract business. In fact, there is evidence that raising prices can increase sales.

- Do not even think about price wars. You cannot win them – not long term. Price wars are destructive and unprofitable. They can ruin your business and damage your industry.

- Discounters can be profitable but not just because they have lower prices. They usually have a lower cost structure and are excellent managers of price variation.

Think about it

What evidence do you have about the price sensitivity of your customers?

What are the issues that affect your customers' buying decisions?

What could you do to persuade your customers to pay more than the 'market' price for your products and services?

How could you further differentiate your offerings from those of your competitors?

What could you do to stimulate sales besides lowering your prices?

___

What are the dangers for you in entering a price war? What could you lose? Could you win one?

___

Have you been a believer of any of these myths? What has it cost you to believe them?

___

Which beliefs will you now abandon? What will you do differently?

___

Chapter 3
Some truths about pricing

"We hold these truths to be self-evident."
American Declaration of Independence

In reality, there are few truths about pricing. There are some great urban legends however, which are held by both consumers ("I always buy the cheapest") and businesspeople ("Lower prices stimulate demand") alike. But as these proclamations come under scrutiny, their truth seems to fade. For example, research shows that customers who claim to buy on price, often do not know how the price of what they purchased compared with the prices of competing products. Sometimes, they cannot even remember how much they paid! But they certainly believe they bought the cheapest product available. By the same token, although it seems to make sense that lower prices stimulate demand, no one really knows to what degree this is true. Perhaps a sale just encourages people to buy now, instead of later. Perhaps it does genuinely increase demand. But does it increase profits? And if so, is it by as much as we think?

Nevertheless, there are a few truths about pricing, although we should keep in mind that the German philosopher Nietzsche once said: "Truths are illusions whose illusionary nature we have forgotten." I think this means that we made up the truth and then forgot that we made it up!

"Truths are illusions whose illusionary nature we have forgotten."
Nietzsche

Truth #1: Price is a factor

There is no doubt that price is a factor in the buying decisions of both business customers and consumers alike. For that reason, generally speaking your price must be within the market range for the market segment you are targeting. In my experience, this means that your price should be no more than 15 - 20% higher than your competitors' prices. This is not a hard and fast rule, but any more than that and you have probably moved into a different segment of the market.

Business people suffering from Mad Price Disease cannot imagine that you could win any business at all if your price is even slightly higher than your competitors'. This is true, unless of course your product or service contains more value than your competitors' offerings. Then price becomes less of a factor. So, we pay a few percent more to shop at the corner store because it is more convenient. We pay many percent more to buy label clothing or to eat in fancy restaurants because it makes us feel good. We pay more for airline tickets because we belong to a loyalty program. We pay more to deal with a plumber or lawyer because we know and trust them. The list is endless. Indeed, the more value you create, the more the price factor diminishes. If you were suffering from cancer, for example, and Acme Drug's product was 50% more effective than anything else on the market, you would probably pay 50% more for it. The point is, that it is relatively easy to persuade your customers to pay 1- 4% more, quite possible to get them to pay 5-15%, but a real big ask to get them to pay 25% more, unless you have created significantly more value than your competitors.

Price is a factor but it is not the main factor. I have recently worked with a number of companies who have asked their customers how important price is in their buying decision and it typically comes out as the third most important issue. Occasionally it is the second, but rarely is it the first. Nevertheless, price is an issue. In fact in this crowded marketplace, you can expect to be attacked on price particularly if you are a market leader. Your job is to neutralize the price issue and turn it to your advantage (See Chapters 7 and 8). You do have a choice about how you will compete in this very competitive market place. You can compete on price, or you can compete on value. But be clear

If you do not compete on value, you will have no alternative but to compete on price.

about this, if you do not compete on value, you will have no alternative but to compete on price.

Truth #2: Lower prices have a place in businesses

Lower prices, discounts and sales do have a place in business. Sales and discounts, for example, are useful for clearing perishable, obsolete or excess stock, or to stimulate demand for slow moving goods. Occasional sales can stimulate buying in slow periods or encourage people to spend more than they had planned to spend. Offering lower prices is also a useful strategy when you are starting a new business, trying to break into a new market segment or introducing a new product or service. It is also a good way to increase market share, providing that you can turn that market share into profitable business in the future. Many companies have discovered that buying market share does not improve profitability.

Discounts are also appropriate when you are able to obtain or produce your products and services at a low cost. Whenever I publish a new book, for example, I offer a number of valued clients a pre-publication special price. This offer looks like it provides the customer with a discount but it is a discount that does not cost me anything (except arguably an opportunity cost) because I add these sales to the number of books I had planned to print. These run-ons, of course, cost next to nothing to produce but on some occasions I have been able to fund the entire print run from pre-publication sales. This helps the cash flow no end!

Low prices can increase profitability in businesses which have high fixed costs. For these companies, the additional sales provide the cream, even if the margins are lower. Airlines and manufacturers with big investments in plant, or large consulting firms or retail stores with large numbers of staff for example, have high costs of operation even if they carry no passengers, manufacture no products or sell no services or merchandise. These companies benefit from lower prices if those prices stimulate demand because the better their utilization rate, the cheaper the unit cost.

As we have seen, some companies can go beyond offering occasional low prices to being able to offer every day low pricing and still remain profitable. This is because they have created a completely different cost structure from anyone else in their industry. Southwest Airlines, for instance, is one of the most consistently profitable airlines in the world, and that is no mean feat when most of the world's airlines are on the brink of bankruptcy. A major part of Southwest Airlines' success comes from having lower prices than their competitors. But Southwest is able to do that because, being a relative newcomer to the industry, they have a very different cost structure. They fly only one type of aircraft, thereby reducing purchasing, maintenance and operating costs. They

---

Lower prices have their place

Sales and discounts are useful for:

- clearing perishable, obsolete or excess stock.
- stimulating demand for slow moving goods.
- stimulating buying in slow periods.
- attracting customers to your business.
- encouraging people to spend more.

Offering lower prices is a useful strategy when:

- starting a new business.
- trying to break into a new market segment.
- introducing a new product or service.
- attempting to increase market share.
- increasing utilization in a high fixed cost business.

Every day low prices work when you:

- have a cost advantage over your competitors.
- are good at managing price variation.

fly out of a hub and offer a no-frills service, thereby further reducing operating costs. Other more traditional airlines cannot match this cost structure and many have learned at considerable expense that they cannot compete with Southwest on price. Certainly they can match Southwest's fares, but not for long. Southwest's cost advantage means that the lower fares cause the traditional carriers to lose money whereas Southwest is profitable at that price.

Lower prices do have a place in business, but offering low prices is always a risky strategy. Discounting, low prices and sales affect the stability of your base or every day price. Often customers come to expect to be able to buy at the reduced price all the time. A definition of value that professional valuers often use is, *"Value is the lowest price the seller is prepared to accept and the highest price the purchaser is prepared to pay."* You should be aware that when you discount, you are in effect saying, "This is really the lowest price I am prepared to accept."

When your customers hear you say that, they ask themselves, "If this is the lowest price this company is prepared to accept, why should I ever again pay more?" You will find that hard to answer once you have set a precedent of accepting a discounted price. The next thing you know, your margins and revenues are heading down and your costs are heading up. Scary thought!

> "Continuous discounting or underpricing a high quality brand can completely reposition that brand and train consumers to believe that the value of the brand is at the lower price over time."
>
> *Mark Barr, managing director of Marketing & Innovation, Goodman Fielder*

Truth #3: Performance affects price

Now this is a truth! So much so, that when people complain about the price, they are often complaining about their supplier's performance.

> ## The attraction of promotions
>
> Without a doubt, there are some things that short-term price promotion can accomplish. Here's the most popular list of reasons we have heard:
>
> - Shift stock (by giving the product away).
> - Help catch up on a missed sales target (at a cost).
> - Postpone losing shelf space (until the next threat).
> - Buy extra shelf space (for a time).
> - Help keep up with the competition (they did that last week).
> - Have something to do (instead of going to see the agency).
>
> *David Ogilvy on Pricing*

You do not mind paying for something (even bank fees!) if you then get the value you expected to get from the product or service. But when the bank does not transfer the funds into your partner's bank account as you requested, and their EFTPOS card does not work as a result, then no price is low enough to compensate for the wrath of an irate spouse!

There is research to support the claim that performance affects price. Two studies from America, one in the banking industry and one with airlines, produced identical results. The researchers took a sample of customers and allocated them into one of several categories: those who had had 0-1 problems with their bank or airline during the previous year, those who had had 2-3 problems, and so on up to those who had experienced more than 10 problems. The results showed that virtually none of the customers who had 0-1 problems were dissatisfied with the prices they paid, a small percentage of those experi-

Are customers complaining about price or performance?
Bank fees worry clients

Bank fees are excessive and banks don't give consumers enough information about their fees, say callers on 0800 numbers.

0800 Bankline was set up last year by the Consumer Affairs Ministry to gauge banking customer satisfaction. Its findings show people want a clearer explanation of how bank fees reflect costs, fees itemised on bank statements and specific fees for transactions to be fully disclosed before the transaction, he says.

Bankline received 1358 calls, with the majority about fees and service.

Many callers perceived a lack of competition between banks with fees and service and were suspicious that fees charged did not reflect costs and many callers commented on the lack of transparency in fee charging.

Most callers consider bank fees to be excessive and that they represent a high cost to small business owners, low income earners and beneficiaries.

Some self-declared middle and high income earners also commented on the high cost of fees.

There were several complaints about service with callers perceiving a decline in personal service and that loyalty wasn't valued.

Other concerns with banks' service included long waits, not being able to phone their local branch and bank staff having inadequate knowledge of products.

A caller said staff at his bank didn't know what constituted a management fee.

Business to Business

Petrol pricing messy

A weekend petrol price blitz in which up to 16¢ a litre was shaved off premium fuel confused motorists and even the oil companies.

Shell admits its latest cut-price promotion got messy after its competitors first matched, then bettered, the oil company's offer of high-grade 96 octane petrol at the 91 octane price – essentially a 5¢ a litre cut for 96 octane.

As the price skirmishing escalated during the weekend, Mobil shifted the price of both grades of petrol down 5¢ a litre, undercutting Shell, which then dropped 96 octane a further 5¢ a litre to keep both grades at the same price.

BP then entered the battle, chopping prices by 10¢ a litre on both grades. That forced Shell to cut 96 octane petrol by a further 5¢, a total reduction of 15¢ a litre, to honour its promise to keep both grades at the same price for the weekend.

Oil company spokesmen were unable to tell The Press exactly what their prices were without checking yesterday.

The Christchurch Press

encing 2-3 problems complained about the price, and nearly all those who had encountered 10+ problems thought they had paid too much. The message is clear. You must get the basics right before trying to persuade your customers to pay more.

This research also has another lesson. If your customers are complaining about your prices, perhaps it is your performance they are unhappy with. Reducing your price is not going to solve your customer's problem, but it will create some for you. I encountered an example of this the other day. I was looking at buying a new car and was finding the whole experience very frustrating because the car salesmen wanted to show me cars without first discovering what it was I valued. At the end of one particularly trying Saturday afternoon, I was negotiating to buy a vehicle and I mentioned to the manager of the car yard that not once during all the days that I had been shopping around, had any of the salespeople I had been dealing with asked me what I was looking for in a car, not even his salesperson. To my embarrassment, he called in his salesman and told him this in such a way that the salesman could not have failed to feel belittled and humiliated. After an awkward silence in which the salesman and I both wished we were someplace else, the manager added, "So you'd better take him back out on the lot and show him some cheaper cars." If there had ever been even the slimmest chance that I would buy a car from these people if I lived to be 100, it disappeared in a flash.

Satisfaction with performance affects satisfaction with price.

Truth #4: Simple is best

Research shows that when it comes to pricing, simple is best. Unfortunately, most companies, and government agencies for that matter, have moved towards more complex pricing models in the last few years as they have tried to disguise what people really pay for their goods and services. There was a time when you could tell at a glance how much you paid central government in taxes, local government in rates, and businesses such as banks in fees. But today,

> "The user-pays principle bites deeply with customers because they are using an intangible. When they have to buy a transaction in a bank, the perception that they are getting value is diminished, so it is very important that customers perceive they are getting value."
>
> *John McFarlane, CEO, ANZ Bank (Australia)*

thanks to 'user pays' pricing models, it is hard to know just what many goods and services are really costing. How much, for example, do you pay the central government each year? Add up what you pay in income tax, ACC, GST, road-user charges (in the price of petrol), taxes built in to alcohol and tobacco products, and other user-pay fees and you will agree with the man who suggested the income tax form could be simplified to two lines: What did you earn last year? Send it in!

Not surprisingly, there is a growing backlash among consumers and business customers, alike. They want transparency in pricing. They want to know what they are really paying. Indeed, research shows that complex pricing models turn customers off. This is a lesson that the large telecommunications companies in the United States have learned over the past few years. As they tried to find more creative ways of stealing each other's customers, they created more and more complex pricing models. Finally, the consumer went into overload and refused to switch.

The lesson is to keep the pricing simple. Make it easy for people to understand what they are paying and what they get in return. I will say repeatedly, your customers do not want low prices, they want great value. How can they work out the value they are getting if they cannot easily compare the benefits they receive with the costs they pay? Moreover, hidden costs, by definition, come as a surprise. Your customers do not want surprises. They learned years ago that 90% of all surprises in business are bad!

Truth #5: You will have to sell more

If you lower your prices and do not reduce your costs, you must increase your sales to maintain your profitability. Most companies reduce their prices to increase their turnover, yet they have no idea about how much that turnover must increase to cover the reduction in margin. Do you? When you do understand this number, you may find that the increase in sales required is too much to be having a sale or giving a discount. The table on the next page, produced by Results Corp in Queensland is a useful guide to calculating how much your sales would have to increase to compensate for a price reduction, assuming your costs remain the same and you wish to maintain your current level of profit.

Would you like wheels with that?

And you reduce your price by	If your present margin is								
	20%	25%	30%	35%	40%	45%	50%	55%	60%
	To produce the same profit your sales volume must increase by								
2%	11%	9%	7%	6%	5%	5%	4%	4%	3%
4%	25%	19%	15%	13%	11%	10%	9%	8%	7%
6%	43%	32%	25%	21%	18%	15%	14%	12%	11%
8%	67%	47%	36%	30%	25%	22%	19%	17%	15%
10%	100%	67%	50%	40%	33%	29%	25%	22%	20%
12%	150%	92%	67%	52%	43%	36%	32%	28%	25%
14%	233%	127%	88%	67%	54%	45%	39%	34%	30%
16%	400%	178%	114%	84%	67%	55%	47%	41%	36%
18%	900%	257%	160%	106%	82%	67%	56%	49%	43%
20%	-	400%	200%	133%	100%	80%	67%	57%	50%
25%	-	-	500%	250%	167%	125%	100%	83%	71%
30%	-	-	-	600%	300%	200%	150%	120%	100%

*Ref: Results Corp, QLD

Truth #6: Your customers WILL pay more.

This is the hardest truth for people to accept. I see people struggling with this truth in the seminars I run. They want to learn how to persuade their customers to pay more but try as they might, they just do not believe that it can be done. When I see this I ask people this question: "What do you spend your money on today, that five years ago you would not have dreamed of buying?" One of the most common answers I get is, "Water." Imagine if five years ago I had come to you and asked you

What do your customers spend their money on today, that five years ago they would not have dreamed of buying?

to invest $50,000 in a new business to sell water to New Zealanders! You would probably have laughed at the idea. After all, it is not as if we have a shortage of pure fresh water. But look at how large that industry is today. The other day, I heard on the radio that educating overseas students in New Zealand is one of the top 10 earners of overseas funds, several times larger than the wine industry. Who would have thought that five years ago?

Not only do you not have to discount your prices in order to win business, you can even put your prices up. But most business people are afraid to ask their customers to pay more. Fear, not logic, is what stops businesspeople from increasing prices. Fear that their customers will argue the price and they will not know how to counter their objections. Fear that their customers will refuse to pay the higher prices and take their business elsewhere. Fear that their superiors will complain about the lack of sales and they will have no justification for the poor results. People agree to discounts because they are afraid to lose the sale. Better to get 80% of the price than nothing, is the thought that goes through most people's heads. It is easier to justify not getting the full price than it is to explain why you missed the sale. "Customers aren't prepared to pay that much," we can always tell the boss. "Our competitors are selling for less. We have to meet the market." It is

Fear, not logic, is what stops us from increasing our prices.

Cheap books on the web? Fiction

Prices haven't been cut to the bone.

In fact, prices of the *Times* best-sellers and random titles both tended to rise a bit. Apparently, some e-tailers, under pressure to become more profitable, realized they could lower their discounts (i.e. raise their prices) and still attract customers.

BusinessWeek

worth learning to overcome that fear. Retail sales in New Zealand for January 2001 were up 7% over sales for January 2000. Price increases, however, accounted for 4% of that growth in revenue. Had retailers been too frightened to increase their prices then the increase would have barely kept pace with inflation.

Raising your prices is not nearly as difficult as most people think. A few months ago I was talking to a couple who owned a grocery store. They had been listening to a speech I had been giving on business success and afterwards they approached me and asked for some advice about running their business. It seemed that earnings had dropped significantly over the past year and they wondered if I had any ideas about what they could do. I asked them what they knew about their customers and they told me that most of them came in between 4pm and 6pm and typically purchased food for their dinner. "It sounds to me like they are convenience shopping," I said. "In that case, what will matter most to your customers will be that you have plenty in stock and a good variety of foods, too." I told them that I doubted price would be the issue so I suggested they increased their prices. For the next two hours we discussed whether they could do this. They readily admitted they were frightened to increase their prices in case trade dropped off further. Finally, I had exhausted all my arguments. "I've told you all I can," I said. "The next move is up to you."

Aim to have 10% fewer customers.

Four months later, I happened to run into the couple quite by chance. "Well, we did what you suggested," they told me. "One Friday night, after the staff had gone home, we got some friends over and we re-priced everything in the store. We put all the prices up 3%. We didn't tell anyone that we had done this, not even the staff, and do you know what? Nobody noticed! Not one customer said anything. Not even the staff appeared to notice the increased prices. But we can see a difference because our revenue is on track to increase $80,000 per year!" A few weeks later I was telling this story to the CEO of one of New Zealand's larger companies. "That's interesting," he said when I had finished, "because last year we agonized over increasing the price of one of our major products. Finally we took the plunge and sales went up. Not just revenue, but sales!" A small increase in your price will not cause customers to flee, but it will make a big difference to your bottom line.

When I tell this story, I often have people say to me, "Well now that you mention it, we actually put our prices up last year and no one noticed either." When we think of increasing our prices we automatically think of those customers who will resist. We can just see their faces and hear their objections. We know it will be a tough sell. But the 80/20 rule tells us that 80% of your sales or revenue will come from 20% of your customers, and it is these customers who are least likely to complain about, or even notice, a price increase. By putting up your prices you might lose some customers but they will likely be the low margin, low profitability customers. Perhaps you would be better off without them? Here is a crazy thought: What if your target for next year was to have 10% fewer customers but to be getting 5% higher prices from those you retained? It is not such a zany notion. Many company directors and senior managers are beginning to realize that enough attention has been paid to cost cutting and now it is time to shift the focus to the top line.

The question is not, "Will my customers pay more?" but "What would I have to do to get my customers to pay more?"

Truth #7: Price is not a fixed point

Often discussions about pricing give the impression that price is a fixed point in objective reality. In fact, it is not. First of all, price is as much about perception as about reality. Everyone wants a bargain, but what is a bargain? One customer's idea of a bargain is another's idea of wasting money, or yet another customer's idea of price gouging. It all depends on the customer's view of value.

What constitutes a good price also varies with the customer's expectation. One study, for example, found that customers were more willing to pay $20 for a CD when the CDs were placed near sweatshirts that were priced at $80 than when the CDs were placed near sweatshirts that were only $10, *even though the people buying the CDs had no interest in buying the sweatshirts.* Most customers believe that they are rational shoppers yet their perception of price is affected by past experience, advertising messages, and even the price of unrelated products. Therefore you should put your most expensive items at the front of your catalogue or at the top of your price list or invoice. The prices of the less expensive items further down the list will appear cheap by comparison, even though those prices might be higher than the customer could obtain elsewhere.

Setting the price just below a price barrier makes it look inexpensive.

Prices, of course, are not fixed points. They fall in a band. Nearly everyone in business is familiar with the concept of price breaks but many do not realize that once you have gone through a price barrier, you are better off to go well past it and set the price close to the next barrier. For example, if you decide to increase your price from $9.95, once you go through the $10 barrier, do not set the price at $11.95 or even $13.95. It will be more likely that your customer will purchase the offering if you charge $14.95. This is because setting the price just above the $10 price barrier makes it look expensive, whereas setting it just below the $15 price barrier makes it look inexpensive, according to Australian retail consultant, John Stanley.

> Any fool can reduce the price. It takes skill, faith and perseverance to compete on value.

Summary

- There are only a few truths about pricing and those should be viewed with skepticism.

- **Truth #1** Price is a factor, but it is not the main factor. It is your job to neutralize the price issue.

- **Truth #2** Sales, discounts and lower prices do have a place in business. They can all increase turnover. That increased turnover comes at a cost, however. Know what that cost is likely to be before you reduce your prices.

- **Truth #3** Performance affects price. If your customers encounter poor product or service quality they will complain about the price.

- **Truth #4** Simple is best. Customers do not like complex pricing models and they hate hidden fees and charges. Be transparent in your pricing.

- **Truth #5** If you want to maintain your margins after you have reduced your price, you will have to sell more unless you can reduce your costs. Find out how much more before you lower your prices.

- **Truth #6** Your customers will pay more. In fact, it is easier to say no to discounts, or even increase your prices than you think.

- **Truth #7** Price is not a fixed point. Rather it is a band. Set your price just under a price barrier not just over one.

Think about it

Where are you offering discounts, low prices and sales?

What benefits are you getting from these?

What is it costing you to get these benefits?

Are they worth it?

How could your pricing strategy be improved?

What performance problems do you have that might be causing customers to complain about price?

Chapter 4
Customer value is everything

"Everything is worth what its purchasers will pay for it."
Publilius Syrus, 1 BC

It is a beautiful autumn morning as the plane slips through the clear blue sky on its final approach. Great, I think, for it looks like we might be on the ground five minutes early. This is important because the client I am on my way to see always schedules the first meeting for 0930. Even if the plane does arrive at the scheduled time of 0910, this still gives me only 20 minutes to drive 30km from the airport to the small town where they are based. Not an easy task since the roads are windy and often wet. But today they will be dry and I will have an extra five minutes to drive at a more leisurely speed.

In good humour, I stride into the small provincial terminal to collect my rental car, which had been reserved several weeks earlier, only to be told there is no car available for me. It seems the car they had intended to give me was unexpectedly dropped off the night before in a different town. Valuable minutes slip through my fingers as I listen to the manager make feeble excuses and deliver unnecessarily long explanations, which are designed to save face of course. When she is finished apologising she pauses, and the look on her face tells me she hopes I will rescue her by coming up with a solution. Perhaps she thinks I will tell her that I do not mind about the car and that I will be happy to get back on the plane and go home! Perhaps she thinks I would enjoy the walk. When I say nothing, she suggests the rental company will pay for a taxi to take me to my destination. Then later in the day, she tells me, they will deliver the car to where I am working

"I'm sorry Dr Brooks but we don't have a car for you today."

so I can drive back to the airport. "That sounds fine to me," I say encouragingly.

We walk outside where another couple of minutes are lost talking to the only taxi sitting at the airport. Unfortunately, he is booked. More minutes evaporate as the taxi company is rung. Fifteen minutes later a taxi arrives from town and I am finally on my way, but by now it is 0935. At last I arrive at my client's but I am late, of course, 25 minutes late in fact. As I make apologies to the people I have kept waiting, I think to myself that the really annoying thing is that this situation did not have to turn out like this. It would have been different if the car rental company had understood that I did not want one of their cars, I simply wanted to get to my client's. Because the company did not understand that, they wasted valuable time worrying about the car and making apologies for not having one. Had the company understood the value I was looking to get from their product, they would have had a taxi waiting when I arrived. Then, when I got off the plane, they would have briefly explained the situation, and held the door open while I jumped into the waiting taxi. A disappointing experience would have been transformed into a delightful one since not only would I have had lots of time and a lovely sunny day, but I would have been chauffeured as well.

Creating value is what you get paid to do

In *Second To None: Six Strategies for Creating Superior Customer Value*, I suggested that business is the activity of creating value. Two and half years and over a thousand audiences later, I am even more convinced that creating customer value is not just important to your business, it is your business. Creating value is what you get paid to do. Your customers do not want your products and services; they want what your products and services will do for them. It is essential that everyone in your organisation understands this because in a crowded and competitive market, those who deliver value best will prosper, and those who do not will fall by the wayside.

Your customers do not want your products and services; they want what your products and services will do for them.

> Businesses that achieve a superior customer value proposition have average profit margins on sales that are three times greater than those businesses that have an inferior customer value proposition. Research demonstrates that enhancing customer value has a direct impact on the bottom line of an organisation.
>
> *Quality Progress*

This is why the first step to persuading your customers to pay more is to deliver more value than your competitors. In fact, you will not persuade your customers to pay more if you do not offer value because how well a company creates, sells and delivers value has a direct impact on the prices people are prepared to pay. A Gallup survey of 1000 bank customers conducted in America in 1994, for instance, found that 49% of bank customers believed banking fees were too high. These customers were not complaining about the size of the fees, however, they were really complaining about the lack of value they were receiving. The amount of money they were paying did not seem appropriate given the benefits they believed they were receiving. The proof of this is that in the same survey, 20% said they had changed banks recently because of poor customer service, followed by fees and interest rates. These customers were saying, "Where is the value?"

Understand what your customers are buying

It is a lot easier to create and communicate value if you understand what your customers are buying. As we saw with the car rental company, most companies do not. They are focused on their product or service, not on the value their customers are looking to receive. I was once running a strategic planning session with the directors and executives of a major oil company, and I asked them what business they were in.

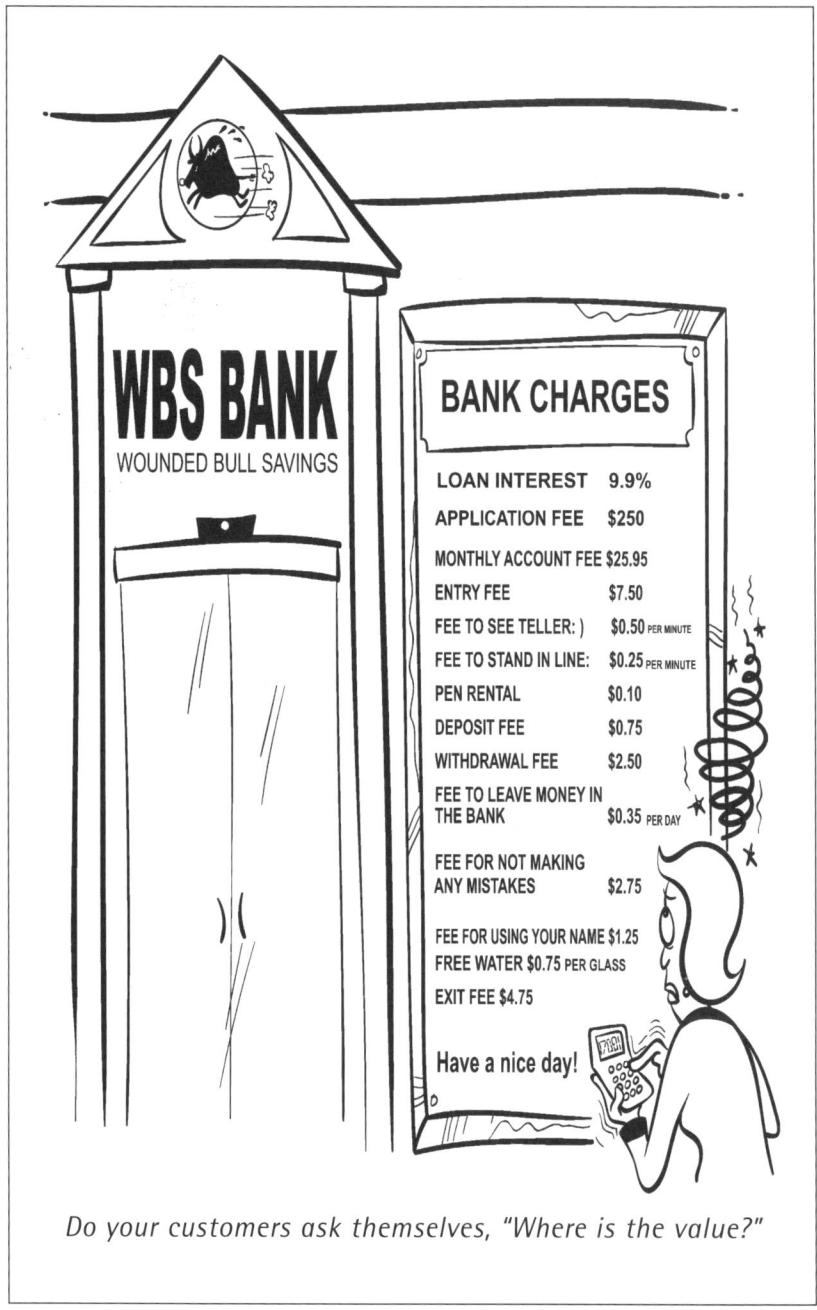

Do your customers ask themselves, "Where is the value?"

"We're in the oil business of course," the CEO said looking at me as if I'd completely lost the plot.

"I don't think so," I replied, confirming his suspicion.

"Listen boy, we spend a lot of time and money looking for oil. When we find it, we recover it. When we recover it, we refine it. And when we have refined it, we sell the refined products. We are in the oil business!" he explained.

"Okay, okay," I said. "That makes sense. The trouble is," I told him, "I've never met anyone who got up in the morning and said: 'Yippee! Today I get a chance to buy 50 litres of petrol.' Who wants the stuff? Even if you could afford it, it's toxic and it stinks! What people want is to drive into town and go to work; or get their boat out on the harbour and chase some fish; or start the lawn mower and tidy up the section because the relatives are coming over. They don't want petrol. They want what the petrol can do for them."

Do you understand what your customers are buying?

The car rental company thought they were in the business of renting cars when they were really in the business of getting people where they want to go. The oil company thought it was in the oil business when its customers were looking for transportation, warm homes or tidy gardens. Car dealers think they are selling cars, when their customers are buying transportation, safety, luxury, or status. City, district and regional councils think they are in the business of local government, while their customers are looking for quality of life. Telephone companies think they are selling telecommunications, while their customers want to be connected. Do you understand what your customers are buying?

If you want to persuade your customers to pay more you must make creating customer value the main focus of your business, because customers make buying value the main focus of *their* business. To create superior value you must first understand the concept of value, and then you must understand what exactly it is that your customers value.

Sell what your customers buy.

What is value?

Value, of course, is subjective and ultimately can only be determined by the customer. Age, gender and situation will affect perception of value, as will previous experience or what people have heard from others. But human beings do not differ from each other as much as we would like to think. Being members of the same gene pool, we share the same physical and mental characteristics, and we also inhabit the same physical environment. Really, we have more in common than sets us apart. Therefore, we can have a generic understanding of value. **Value = Benefit − Cost.** I believe this simple but powerful equation can be used to guide your business activities, to understand your customers' purchasing decisions and to determine your pricing strategy.[1]

> *The real issue is always value. Would you buy a hamburger simply because it was cheap, regardless of how it tasted?*

---

1. For more information about creating superior customer value, see *Second to None: Six Steps for Creating Superior Customer Value* by Ian Brooks, Nahanni Publishing, Auckland, 1997.

Benefits solve problems

People go shopping because they have a *need*. If they have a need that is not met, they have a *problem*. Thus when they go shopping they are looking for a *solution* to that problem. Benefits are features of your product or service that your customers believe will solve their problem. Your main business strategy should be to deliver more benefits to your customers and prospective customers than your competitors could offer. The more you understand your customers problems and the more willing you are to invent solutions to those problems, the more value you will create and the less price will be an issue.

Customers do not want to hear the word, 'no'.

What many businesspeople fail to understand is that their customers' problems are the only reason they have a business. For example, when I was building my new house, I employed two teams of builders to work on the project. They did a great job but after they had finished and moved on to another job, I noticed a small leak. Since one of the gangs was working nearby, I went over to see them. It was lunchtime when I arrived and they were sitting in the sun reading the paper enjoying their lunch. "John," I said to the team leader, "I have a small problem."

"Well, don't bring your problems around here," he said in all seriousness.

What was he really saying to me? He was saying, "I don't want your business!"

Of course you and your people are much too smart to say that to your customers, but how often does someone in your company say no?

"Sorry, mate, we cannot deliver that today."

"No, we don't do that work."

"No, I don't know who does stock that product."

"No, I don't know who you would call to find that information."

"No, you can't pay that way."

"No, we can't put that information on the invoice."

61

Customers do not want to hear the word 'no'. They come to you because they have a problem and, therefore, what they are looking for is a solution. Customers understand that you might not have the solution they are looking for, but in that case, they expect you will help them find somebody who can. Value is either created or destroyed. There is no neutral position. When you say 'no' you destroy value because your customer has invested the time and effort in coming to you but has gained nothing from it. They have paid costs but received no benefits. Thus, as far as they are concerned, the value account is in overdraft.

> "Virtually every operator who has come to pitch for our business turns up with a price list, not wanting to understand our business needs or prepared to look at ways to solve our problems."
>
> Len Morrison, partner with Accenture.
> Morrison buys telephone services for 70,000 people in 46 countries. Quoted in The Times, 26/1/01

If you want to create superior customer value, you must be a can-do person who understands that the only reason they have a business at all is because their customers have problems they are prepared to pay to have solved. You must understand that your choice is to help your customers solve their problems or not help them. But you must also understand that if you choose not to help your customers, their problems do not disappear. You have simply lost an opportunity to create value. In fact, not only have you lost an opportunity to create value, you have created an opportunity for your competitors. No opportunity in business is really ever lost. If you fumble the ball, there is always someone coming along behind you to scoop it up.

If you choose not to help your customers, their problems do not disappear.

Customers do not want to hear 'no' but it is equally dangerous to say 'yes.' This is because customers do not usually tell you the problem

CUSTOMER VALUE IS EVERYTHING

The psychology of buying

All people are driven by needs

A need that is not met becomes a problem.

Your customer's problem is your reason for being in business.

People go shopping for SOLUTIONS

Any feature of your product or service that solves their problem will be perceived as a BENEFIT.

Any feature that does not solve the customer's problem will be seen as waste.

Anything customers must expend - money, time and effort - will be seen as a COST

Customers will see value and buy if they believe the BENEFITS EXCEED THE COSTS

63

they are trying to solve, they just ask for a solution. They might be asking for the wrong solution, of course, since they do not know your business as well as you do. A good rule of thumb is that the customer is always right about the problem they have, but often wrong about the best solution. If you simply give your customer the solution they ask for, and it is the wrong one, you could be in trouble because when they discover the solution does not work, they will blame you. Therefore, before saying either 'yes' or 'no' to your customers, ask questions that will help you understand the problem they are trying to solve. You might say, for example, "We can certainly do that for you but before we do, let me ask you a silly question. Why do you want that? How will it help you?" When you hear their answer you might find yourself saying, "If that is what you want to accomplish, you might find that this solution would work better."

The customer is always right about the problem but often wrong about the best solution.

If you are selling business to business, your customers are buying your products and services for only one reason, and that is to increase the money they make. Thus they are buying (and so you had better be selling) enhanced profitability. The key to creating superior value then, is to understand your business *and* to understand your customers' businesses. How many of us can say that we do? The National Association of Purchasing Managers in the United States undertook a survey of their members and found the 75% believed their suppliers did not understand their business. Comments came back such as, "My suppliers do not understand enough about my business to have an intelligent conversation with me." If you went to visit one of your customers and you did not talk about your products and services, the weather or the latest sports result, could you hold an intelligent conversation with them? Most of us know a lot about how our customers buy and use our products and services but we know little about their businesses. We do not know what their objectives are, which strategies they plan to use to achieve those objectives, and which problems stand in their way.

This point also applies even if you are selling directly to consumers. When consumers buy, they do so in order to maintain or improve their lifestyle. Thus, they are really buying (and, again, we had better be selling) quality of life. Just as with business customers, if you want to make your consumer customers successful, you must discover their goals, understand what they are trying to do to achieve those goals, and identify the obstacles that are in their way. Whether you are selling lifestyle to consumers or enhanced profitability to business customers, the more you learn about your customers' problems the better, because each problem is an opportunity for you to create customer value.

Creating superior value

British Airports Authority turned Heathrow's Terminal 4 into an enticing arcade filled with the world's most elegant shops. Starbucks turned the humble cup of joe into a trendy social event. British based Pret A Manger created a chain of sandwich shops that, with fare like chicken-and-grape baguettes and Moroccan couscous salad, offer a wonderful alternative to burgers and fries. And Southwest Airlines got *everybody flying*.

Sales and Marketing Management

Reduce the costs

The next step to creating superior value is to deliver these solutions at a lower cost than anyone else, but that does not mean reducing your price. Quite the contrary. If you can reduce the cost of ownership by developing something that is easy to use, requires low maintenance or will last longer, the purchase price will start to look cheap even though it is higher than the price of competing products. If you can reduce important non-financial costs such as time (by being fast), effort (by being convenient), or emotional costs (by being reliable and offering guarantees), you can charge more than your competitors do. Have you ever paid more to have a film developed quickly? Or shopped at a corner dairy (where you know the prices are higher) because it was more convenient? Would you pay a little more for a car you thought was more reliable than a cheaper one?

The easier you make it for your customers to do business with you because you are fast, convenient and hassle-free, the more value they will perceive they are getting, and the easier it will be to persuade them to pay more. A good question to ask yourself is whether your business is working for your customers, or whether through your policies, procedures and the way you do things you are making your customers work for you. Again, anything you make your customers do to obtain benefits from your products and services, they will perceive as a cost. The higher these costs are, the less value they will believe they are getting, and the greater the risk you will be seen as a value destroyer, not a value creator. How easy is it for your customers to contact you, for example? "We're sorry, all of our agents are busy right now..." In a crowded and competitive market place, you cannot afford to be destroying value. Your customers will avoid you like the plague.

Give them something extra

To create more value than your competitors, you need to delight your customers by giving them something extra. These delighters are solutions to problems that your customers would just love you to solve but do not really expect that you will. When you do solve them, you knock their socks off!

Delight your customers by giving them something extra.

The taxi industry is a pretty tough business to be in these days. With deregulation in many countries there is a surplus of cabs and price becomes an issue. Taxi drivers work long hours and often have little to show for it at the end of their shift. The trouble is, nearly all taxis look the same and deliver the same range of benefits. Not too long ago

I jumped into a taxi in Toronto, Canada and found myself in a Ford LTD which is a very nice car. The driver was wearing a jacket and tie and looked smart. As we were heading down the freeway into the city he asked me what kind of music I liked to listen to. "Excuse me?" I said.

"What kind of music do you like to listen to, Sir? Tell me and I'll dial it up on the radio. Would you prefer jazz, or rock or pop? Perhaps easy listening, classical or talk-back radio?"

I said classical would be nice and sat back to listen to it.

"Sir," he said. "Since you have just come in to town, you might like to catch up on the local news. There are three daily newspapers in the seat pocket in front of you."

I fished out the Globe & Mail and scanned the headlines.

"Would you like something to drink, Sir?" he asked after a few minutes. "A cup of coffee or tea?"

I said that coffee would be nice.

"Will that be regular or decaffeinated?"

"Regular, please."

"And do you take it black or white?"

"White, thank you."

"Would you prefer cream or milk?"

I chose milk - and, no, I didn't take sugar.

Now I did have to serve myself from the thermos provided. I guess he has not yet learned how to pour coffee while doing 100km/hr down a 16-lane highway but I am sure he is working on it!

I was telling this story at a conference the other day and someone asked me if I paid more for these benefits. I had to admit that I did not know for sure but I imagined I did. But it did not matter to me because the service was so good. On the other hand, it probably mattered to the driver. Another three or four dollars per trip, six or seven times a day, for five or six days a week, for 48 or 50 weeks of the year would add up. And, nearly all of that would be profit because the costs of delivering the benefits were so small. One thing that I am sure of is that when he gave me his card (having determined I would be in town for a week), I did not throw it away as I usually do. After all, why bother keeping them when all taxis are the same? In this case, however, he had demonstrated a difference by delivering superior value and I kept the card - and used him again.

Understand what your customers value

It is very difficult to persuade your customers to pay more if you do not know what they value, and most companies do not. I once asked a senior manager whether his company competed on price or value. "On value, of course," he replied.

"That's great," I said. "What is it that your company does that your customers value?"

After a moment, he grinned. "I haven't got a clue," he said.

Value is what you have that your customer wants and is prepared to pay for.

Value is what you have that your customer wants and *is prepared to pay for*. Most companies overlook this last point. They spend large sums of money finding out what prospective customers would like to buy and whether their existing customers are satisfied, but they do not take the next steps of finding out what people are prepared to pay for and how much they are prepared to pay. Thus they miss seeing opportunities to create value for their customers and for turning that value into profit for themselves. What are your customers prepared to pay for that you are not currently providing? Which features (and therefore costs) are built into your product or service that your customers would not pay for? The answers to these questions could help you to improve the value you are offering your customers - and also the prices you are able to charge.

The more you understand what your customers value, the more profitable you will be. One company that has discovered this is Marriott Lodgings in

America. Marriott operates a chain of five star hotels and a few years ago they decided to build a chain of budget motels. At first, they did the usual market research to discover what their prospective customers were prepared to pay and what they wanted in a budget motel. They established that the going price was US$49 per night but for that amount of money people wanted all the optional features that the market researchers suggested. Clearly, Marriott could not offer all those features, charge only US$49 per night and still make a profit. They decided to run another round of focus groups, but this time they gave participants $49 in play money. They then showed them the basic room layout, said that would cost US$21 and asked participants to put $21 of their play money on the table. They then showed them a list of additional features that could be put in the room and told them how much each would cost. An extra large bathroom, for example, might cost $9 per night, a VCR only $2. The market researchers then asked the participants how they would like to spend their play money. At the end of the exercise they understood not what their prospective customers wanted, but what they were prepared to pay for. Within two years the Marriott motel chain was the most profitable in the country earning profits 26% higher than the industry average.

Understanding what your customers value is a key to being able to persuade your customers to pay more. Even some local governments understand this. One afternoon I happened to be at home when the phone rang. It was a woman from a market research company which had been hired by the local city council, and she asked me if I would answer some questions. I told her that was fine. "Right then, sir, what do you think about the quality of the local beaches?" she asked.

"How many days do we have to talk about this?" I asked in return. She told me we had as long as I wanted so I told her just exactly what I thought about the condition of the local beaches.

"Do you think the local council should do anything to improve the beaches?" she asked. I said I did. Wasn't that why we were talking?

"That's right, sir. It is," she told me. "Would you be prepared to see your rates increase to do this work?" I said I would.

"By $50 a year," she asked. I said yes.

"By $100?" Again I said yes.

"By $150?" I had to think about that but in the end I said yes.

"By $200?"

"No," I told her, that is too much."

"Thank you, sir," she said. "Now, what do you think about the condition of the roads in this city?"

"How many days do we have to talk about this?" I asked and away we went again. The interview went through a number of issues and at the end of every one, I was asked how much I was prepared to pay to have the problem solved. That was brilliant research because at the end of the exercise, management of the local council, and the councillors themselves, understood what their customers wanted and how much they were prepared to pay to get those things. In other words, they understood what their customers valued.

You do have a choice

Your choice is to compete on price or to compete on value. If you do not compete on value, however, you will have no option but to compete on price. Before you take the default option, you should know that competing on price could destroy not only your own profitability but that of your whole industry. Price wars, as we have seen, benefit no one, not even the customer in the long run. There is a better way: Create superior value, attach a fair price to it and sell that value to the consumer. This is your job. The aim of management should be to optimise the long-term sustainable profitability of the company and that comes from striving for the best achievable margin. To create sufficient value that you can persuade your customers to pay more, your entire staff must see that the purpose of your business is to enhance the lives of your customers in some way. You must help them to see beyond the order form, the invoice or the customer complaint to the person at the end of the value chain, the end-user, whose life will be improved by your product or service. You must help everyone to think, indeed worry, about this because that is what your customers worry about. It is what they pay you to do. Every time a customer makes a purchase, they ask themselves: "Do the benefits outweigh the costs?" If the answer is yes, they will go away happy and probably return later to buy more. They may even tell their friends how good you, your product or your service is.

Be on the constant look out for opportunities to create value and exploit them when you find them. In a bleak world, give people hope and create fun. In a complex world, make things simpler and easier. In a time of uncertainty, give advice, guidance and support. When people have too much to do, offer to do some of it for them. When people are trying to fit everything in, offer flexibility. Give people the knowledge, skills and confidence to take control over their lives. Be creative and innovative so that you can give your customers a leading edge. But always remember that creating superior customer value is a never-ending journey because what was seen as extra value yesterday will be taken for granted today - and will be viewed as inadequate tomorrow.

Your choice is to compete on price or to compete on value.

Summary

- Your customers do not want your products and services; they want what your products and services will do for them. They are looking to extract value from your offerings.
- Creating value is what you get paid to do. In a competitive market, those who understand and create value best will prosper. The first step to persuading your customers to pay more, is to deliver more value than your competitors do.
- To create more value you must first understand what your customers are buying so you can sell them what they are buying.
- Value is benefits minus costs. Use this equation to drive your business because it is what drives your customers' decisions to buy.
- Benefits are features of your products and services that solve your customers' problems. The more you understand your customers' problems, the more opportunities you will have to create value. You must understand your business and your customer's businesses.
- Customers go shopping because they have problems. Therefore they want solutions and that takes can-do thinking. They do not want to hear 'no.'
- Costs such as time, effort and emotional or mental costs are 'expensive' to your customers. They destroy value. It is worth money to your customers to have these costs reduced.
- You can create value for your customers by giving them something extra. Delight your customers by providing solutions to problems they would just love you to solve but cannot really expect that you would. When you do, you will knock their socks off.
- To persuade your customers to pay more, you must understand what your customers value. Value is what you have, that your customers want and are prepared to pay for. Most companies understand what their customers want, but not what they are prepared to pay for, or how much they are prepared to pay.
- You do have a choice. You can compete on price or value. If you do not compete on value, you will have to compete on price.

Think about it

Are your staff focused on completing tasks, flogging products or creating value?

Do you understand what your customers are buying? What are they buying?

Which contacts do your customers have with you when they would believe they do NOT get more benefits than costs?

How well do you understand what your customers are trying to achieve, and which problems are in their way?

How often do customers hear the word 'no'? What could you change so they hear 'no' less often?

- What non-financial costs do your customers pay to get your products and services? How could you reduce these?

- Where could you give your customers something extra?

- How could you learn more about what your customers value?

- How could you use this information to be able to persuade your customers to pay more?

The five zones of customer value

Chapter 5
The zones of basic value

Price is the enemy of differentiation

The only person who can determine which features of your products and services will command a higher price is your customer. Therefore, as we discussed in Chapter 4, you should invest a considerable amount of time and money in understanding just what it is your customers value. To their cost, many companies fall into the trap of believing they know what their customers value. Often they get it wrong, and they end up destroying value instead of creating it. For example, appliance manufacturers have invented sophisticated appliances that can do remarkable things. The trouble is, most consumers use only the appliance's basic functions, and that creates a problem for the manufacturers. They need to charge more for their products because it costs them more to build the new features, but their customers do not want to pay a higher price because they do not see any added benefits. Because the appliance manufacturers were wrong about what their customers valued, they have created value drains. Value drains exist when you produce features that cost you more to provide than they are worth to your customers. Needless to say, it is difficult to persuade your customers to pay more if you have built value drains into your products and services.

Avoid value drains – features that cost you more to provide than they are worth to your customers.

Not all benefits are equal, of course. Some aspects of your products and services will be seen by your customers as commodity items, and others as extremely valuable benefits. It will be easier to command higher prices if you wrap the commodity with layers of increasingly valuable benefits. Think of the commodity part of your offering as being like a

75

stone. Then think of wrapping that stone with layers of cloth. The first layer might be cotton, which is not highly valued but is certainly worth more than the bare stone. There might be several more layers of cloth wrapped around the stone with each layer being more valuable than the one before it, until the last layer is silk, the most valuable of all the cloths surrounding the stone. The price of the bare stone would be low and the price of the stone wrapped in cotton a little higher. But the highest price would be paid for the stone wrapped in several layers, with the outer layer being silk. This analogy illustrates what you must do to persuade your customers to pay more. You must wrap the basic parts of your products and services with increasingly valuable layers of benefits.

A useful starting point is to think of benefits as being grouped into five 'zones,' ranging from a 'commodity zone' where price is definitely the issue to the 'platinum zone' where price does not affect the customer's decision to buy. The basic solution which you are providing to your customer is likely to be just a commodity item as far as your customer is concerned because it is no different from that offered by your competitors in their eyes. The only factor affecting their decision to purchase, therefore, is likely to be price. Since you do not want to compete on price, you must wrap your basic solution in layers of benefits that your customers are prepared to pay more for. The more layers or zones of benefits that are wrapped around your basic solution, the more valuable your product or service will be to your customers, and the more you can charge as a result.

The commodity zone – the naked solution

Businesses exist because their customers have one or more problems which they are prepared to pay someone to solve. The most basic zone of value, therefore, contains a naked solution to the customer's problem and little else. This is the commodity zone because a naked solution is always simple, readily available, and no different from anything a competitor can provide. A concrete block is a concrete block. Sugar is sugar. A log is a log. Because there

A naked solution is always simple, readily available, and no different from anything a competitor can provide.

is no difference between one supplier's commodity item and another's, the naked solution has to be offered at a low price.

There was a time when we thought of commodity items as being only those products or services which were either unprocessed or minimally processed, such as logs, sugar and concrete blocks. But today, thanks to the quality revolution of the 1980s and 1990s, consumers see many sophisticated products as being merely commodity items because the level of quality in these products and services is universally good and does not vary across suppliers. Thus within a given price band, cars, computers, couriers, and even hotel rooms are considered to be commodity items. Within a level of performance or luxury, for example, you can name half a dozen makes of cars or chains of hotels that are as good as each other. There is no differentiation. Because prospective purchasers see these products and services as being commodities, the only factor affecting their decision to buy is price. Even professional service firms such as lawyers, consulting engineers and recruitment consultants are in this situation. The other day, I was trying to convince a group of consulting engineers not to compete in tenders on the basis of price. "You don't understand, Ian," one of them wailed. "We have to compete on price because our customers do not see any difference between us and our competitors." Therein lies the problem! Their services are seen as merely a commodity item.

Even professional service firms such as lawyers, consulting engineers and recruitment consultants are seen as commodities.

No matter who you are, if all you are providing your customers is a naked solution, then you will have no option but to compete on price. Remember that utility company I spoke about in Chapter 1 which advertised: *All electricity is the same – except that ours costs less?* What this company is saying to its customers and prospective customers is that the only problem their customers have is sourcing energy, and that the only solution this company can provide, therefore, is electricity - the same electricity as could be purchased from many other energy suppliers. Consequently, this company believes the only reason anyone would buy from them is that their electricity is cheaper. This energy supplier chose to provide only a naked solution and is forced to be a price-taker as a result. Had they wrapped the solution with higher valued benefits such as billing accuracy or customer service (imagine phoning a utilities company and not having to wait for 13 minutes before you could talk to someone!), they might have been price-makers instead. Coca Cola, for example, has explored the development of vending machines that automatically change the price according to the ambient temperature, or according to the number of cans of Coke left in the machine. On a cool day with a machine crammed full of Coke, the price for a can would be very competitive, but you would probably have to sell your car to have enough money to buy the last can of Coke on a sizzling hot day!

Differentiating commodities

Bananas – Brand them. Stick a label on them calling them *Chiquita Bananas*. Dole did the same with pineapple.

Vegetables – Give them human faces and a friend called the *Jolly Green Giant*.

Cantaloupes – Create a new category. Don't just call them big. Call them Crenshaw melons.

Chinese gooseberry – Create an identity. Call it Kiwifruit.

Pig – Pork was just pig for many years. Now it is known as *the other white meat* which appeals to the health conscious.

There is always a way to differentiate!

It is very difficult to produce healthy profits if all you are offering is a naked solution unless you have a monopoly, or an untapped market into which you can expand, because price will always be the issue. Every conversation you have with your customers will be about price – specifically about how you should lower your price. That can be very tiresome! That is why most companies would prefer not to trade in the commodity zone. You can enjoy better margins if you can differentiate your offering from those of your competitors, and the best way to do this is to add layers of benefits which address more of your customer's needs or problems. In other words, you will add increasing value with each successive layer that you wrap around the naked solution. I think there are four zones of differentiation, each worth progressively more to the customer and, therefore, capable of commanding a higher price.

If all you are providing your customers is a naked solution, then you will have no option but to compete on price.

The Bronze Zone

The Bronze Zone involves more than just providing a naked solution to your customer's problem. It means getting the basic transaction right and it involves delivering the basic elements of good customer service. Most importantly, these need to happen consistently, not every now and then. This is not what most customers experience. A recent American study that showed over 80% of customers said good service was an important ingredient in their buying decision but that 41% said they were not getting the service they expected. I get the same result in my own informal polls. I frequently ask audiences to raise their hands if they have had poor customer service within the last two weeks. Typically, 75% do so. Good consistent service, delivered by staff who care, is uncommon, and therefore it is worth paying for in the minds of most customers. One of the problems is that few companies understand what kind of experience their customers are seeking. Or if they do, they forget to tell their staff.

Most customers will pay for good consistent service delivered by staff who care.

What would extra benefits be worth to your customers?

Reliability

A key component of the bronze zone is reliability. Over the years, I have had the opportunity of attending hundreds of formal meetings in which customers have told their suppliers, "Price is important but reliability is even more important." Irrespective of the industry, and no matter which country, the message customers give is the same: They are prepared to pay more for products that work, that have consistent quality and that are delivered in-full and on-time.

Most customers believe that price is important but reliability is even more important.

This makes sense. If you owned a business, would you deal with an unreliable supplier who, although cheaper, kept letting you down? Of course not because that would mean you would fail to keep your commitments to your customers. You could not afford to take the risk that your customers would stick with you in spite of your poor performance. In fact, you *know* they would go somewhere else because sticking with you would mean letting their own customers down. Your customers know that poorly performing products and services from you and their other suppliers can put them out of business. On a personal level, would you pay $8,000 for a car that may well break down during the first year you own it, or would you rather pay $10,000 for a vehicle you are confident will give you 12 to 18 months of worry-free motoring? Reliability is important whether it is product reliability or service reliability. Therefore, if you become a reliable supplier, your customers will perceive you are delivering increased value, and that means you will be able to charge more. Unfortunately most companies do not take advantage of this fact.

Product and service reliability are important because they meet the need for security. If that need is met, your customers will have a feeling of comfort, and because that is exactly the feeling they want to have, your customers will be prepared to pay for it. On the other hand, if your customers' need for security is not met, they will feel anxious. Anxiety is an emotional cost which will reduce your customers' perception of the value they are receiving. If that happens they will, as we have discussed, complain about the price. If you can consistently produce products and services that work as they should, that are delivered on time, in full, as promised; and if you consistently do what you say you are going to do, then you will develop a reputation for reliability. People will come to you because of that reputation, and they will come to you already having decided to buy because of your reputation. Such customers are not so price sensitive.

Product and service reliability are important because they meet the need for security.

Speed and convenience

Two other key components of the Bronze Zone are speed and convenience. Customer research confirms what you know from your own experience, and that is that time and energy are in short supply for most people. As the pace of the world quickens and as more is asked of each of us, we find that time and effort are the most expensive 'prices' we have to pay to purchase something. As a result, your customers will pay a premium for speed and convenience - just like you do. Saving time or energy is quite often worth more to you than the few dollars it costs you. But that extra money can make a big difference to the profitability of your supplier!

Price is important but reliability is much more important.

Speed and convenience are even more important to your customers if you are selling business to business. Time is money, and anything you can do to reduce the work your business customers have to do will save them in labour costs. I was talking to the owner of a collision repair centre recently. He told me that he now dealt with only one paint supplier because it reduced the amount of time his paint shop manager had to spend talking to sales people from other companies. He knew that even if he were paying a little more money for some products, he would still be dollars ahead because of the management time saved. This why many large corporates are rationalizing suppliers. Some will end up dealing with fewer than 10% of their original suppliers.

THE ZONES OF BASIC VALUE

> Last year, 46% of America's family food dollars were spent on meals or snacks outside the home.
>
> 50% of that money went to fast food outlets.

A key aspect of convenience is making it easy for people to do business with you, particularly when it comes to paying you. Make it easy for people to pay and price becomes much less important. The growth of consumer financing is proof of that. I used to make the mistake of discounting my books when I spoke at a conference. Today I charge full retail but I allow people to choose the way they pay. They can pay by cash, cheque, credit card or I will invoice them. Whichever way they choose to pay, they can walk out the door with the books under their arm. What could be easier? I once was given a $50,000 consulting job because someone was so impressed with how easy it was to buy my books that they hired me to help them improve their customers' experience. How easy is it for your customers to pay you? Or to order your products and services? Or to communicate with you? "We're sorry, all of our agents are busy right now ....."

One area involving time that many businesses are not very good at is responsiveness. Your customers are living in a fast-paced world, and therefore they expect that you will return their phone calls, prepare quotes, arrange appointments, send information and respond to product or service problems quickly. A quick response, if sold properly, is worth money to your customers. If you had a major plumbing problem, would you hire a plumber for $40 an hour who can come in three days, or one at $50 per hour who could come today?

Giving your customers easy and quick access to your product or service will affect the demand for them, and therefore the price you can charge. Modern retailing is based on the premise that goods out on the shelves where customers have ready access

A quick response is worth money to your customers.

to them are more easily sold than ones stuck behind the counter. Similarly, studies show that one of the most important satisfaction factors in professional services is accessibility. The world's best lawyer is of no value to you if you cannot get easy access to him. The main attraction of Internet shopping is that a customer can get access to products and services anywhere in the world without leaving home. Credit cards and 0800 numbers have increased people's access to a wide range of products and services through telephone shopping, and television shopping channels and infomercials. Although some of these suppliers are competing on price, many others, such as Amazon.com charge more for their products than people could get from their competitors.

Another area of convenience that is becoming increasingly important is being a one-stop shop. Because we are all so busy, we want the convenience of getting everything we need at one location. The implications of this on pricing are considerable. It means that if through competitive pricing on some items you can attract customers to your business, they will be less concerned about the price of other items they can pick up while they are there. Successful department stores such as Wal-Mart, understand this very well. As I mentioned earlier, Wal-Mart is quite possibly the best manager of price variation in the business. They have loss leaders that bring people into the store and then healthy margins on products people buy on impulse or for convenience. Of course, it would be even better if you could attract people to your place of business for reasons other than price in the first place. Being known as a one-stop shop might just do that.

As workdays get longer and free time gets more precious, people will become increasingly willing to pay for convenience.

The key to being a one-stop shop is to develop strategic partnerships with businesses supplying other products that your customers need so that they can access these through your organisation. Thus, you become the gateway through which they can get many of their problems solved. This would put you in a position of organising the value chain. This is the best position to be in because the gatekeeper is the one who calls the shots and gets the margin as a result. You do not have to be the largest player in the value chain to be the one who controls it. You simply have to be the one who has the relationship with the customer and who best understands the customer's business, needs and problems.

The enemy of convenience is complexity. The world is moving very fast and in many areas, product development is related to what technology can do rather than on what customers want. What is the point of buying a VCR with features you will never figure out how to use? People do not like complexity. Whoever makes it simple will be able to command a premium price. Therefore, your aim should be for simplicity. Simplify your products and services. Simplify how your customers can contact you, simplify the information you provide, simplify the way people do business with you - and charge for it. After all, you are reducing the costs of time and effort when you do and that is worth a lot to your customers.

Personal attention and information

There are times when customers need personal attention and information, and when they do, they will pay for it. Shopping on the Internet is fantastic. As long as you know what you want, it can be fast and very convenient. You never have to leave your desk and you can buy things from a supplier on the other side of the world. The problem comes when you want information, or if a transaction has not proceeded properly. That is when you could really use a real person to talk to, and of course there is never anyone around. Cyberspace, like Outer Space, has a dearth of humans in it. I once got an invoice (electronically, of course) from a company in the USA. I knew I had already paid the account so I emailed them to sort it out. I got an automated reply back saying my message had been received. I had been hoping for a little more than just confirmation they had received my message. I wanted confirmation they knew I had paid the account. So I sent another email: "Please don't give me an automated response. I need to talk to someone about this." You guessed it, back came the same message. No matter what I did, I got the same automated response. I could not contact a live human being. I did fix my problem in the end. I stopped doing business with them.

What's for dinner?

People worldwide are abandoning the home-cooked meal. Here's what the average person spends annually eating out:

 Japan $4,080

 Spain $3,360

 USA $2,246

 Italy $1,980

 UK $1,840

 Canada $1,608

 Germany $1,180

 France $1,120

Amounts are in NZ dollars

You know how frustrating it is to shop in a large store devoid of staff. Who do you ask if you don't know where to find something, or if you don't know the price, or if you need information about a product? At that point, a saving of a few dollars becomes irrelevant. But worse than not being able to find someone is finding an assistant who knows nothing. I am not talking about staff having high-level expertise either. I am referring to staff who have not got a clue about what they are selling. I once asked a salesperson in one of Auckland's oldest and most upmarket department stores for some information about an expensive piece of furniture. "I don't know the answer to that," he said. "I am only in this department for the weekend. I usually work in rugs."

On another occasion I asked the salesperson in one of the country's largest chain of department stores whether I would have trouble tuning

> ## Customers want speedy service – and many will pay for it!
>
> When buyers want help, they want it fast. In a survey of 200 online consumers conducted by Mobius Management, a provider of Web-based data management, nearly 75 percent of respondents said that fast, reliable customer service was key to their selection of a consumer services provider, such as a credit card issuer or mortgage lender. While 86 percent reported they had been forced to wait on hold longer than 10 minutes to speak with a customer service rep in the past, only 32 percent said they would hold that long in the future. And 91 percent said they would change vendors if it consistently took them longer than 10 minutes to connect to a live customer service rep. Half said they'd spend more money for superior customer service.

in a new VCR I was thinking of buying from him since I have Sky Digital. "I don't know," he said. "I don't have Sky."

Once in a restaurant in Australia I asked the maitre d' if a certain white wine was a good one. "I don't know," he said. "I don't drink wine."

In a world where customers are overwhelmed with options, they need guidance in making a choice. They need information. They need advice. They need to talk to staff who are knowledgeable. When they ask someone for assistance, they do not want to hear:

"I'm sorry, I'm new here."

"We just got that product in and I don't know anything about it."

"I don't usually work in this department."

"I'll see if I can find anyone who knows anything about this."

"I only work weekends."

"No, I can't help you, I'm sorry."

If they do, then price will become the main issue. That is, if they shop with you at all.

The quality of the experience your customers have with your staff affects how they feel about the prices you charge.

Remember, approximately 70% of buying decisions are made for emotional reasons, and the quality of the experience your customers have with your staff affects how they feel about your company, your products and services and the prices you charge. It is not just a matter of having someone there who knows something about what you sell either. They must care about helping the customer, too. I went into a bank recently to open a new account. I walked up to the counter and was greeted by the staff member on duty. I told her I would like to open a new account. She looked at me and then she looked at the clock on the wall. "You need two pieces of identification to do that," she said.

I told her that would be no problem. She looked at me and then she looked at the clock on the wall again. "One of them has to have your photo on it."

Again I reassured her that there was no problem since I had my driver's licence with me. She looked at me and looked at the clock on the wall again and sighed deeply. "We really prefer people make an appointment to do this," she told me. There were four competing banks within 500 metres of where we were standing. You would think she would have been pleased to see me. Her CEO certainly thought that.

Many of us, in this fast-moving depersonalised world, are prepared to pay more for personal attention from a competent and caring staff member. It is of value to us to know that someone wants to make our shopping experience a good experience, or even better, is committed to making us successful. I normally deal with a bank that is not the cheapest bank around but I just love it when I ring their telephone banking operation. While nearly every other call centre I deal with conveys the impression that they want to get rid of you as quickly as possible, this call centre ends each call with: "Is there anything else we can do for you today, sir?" It is said in such a relaxed and leisurely way that you feel they are genuinely concerned about helping, and that they have the time to do so.

To provide your customers with the personal attention they would like to have, you must do four things. First, you must have a sufficient number of staff on duty. When you hear a recorded message tell you, "We're sorry, but all of our agents are busy right now. Your call is important to us...," you know they are lying. If your call really was important to them they would have employed enough staff to handle it. What the company has done is cut its costs to the point where it cannot deliver the attention its customers would like. When this happens, customers become disappointed and frustrated. They take their business elsewhere or demand lower prices. Sales drop, and profits shrink so more cost cutting is necessary. It is a vicious circle. I guess running a business that way makes sense to someone. Unfortunately, it is only going to get worse because today's corporate managers seem to be once again obsessed with reducing the head count.

Many customers will pay more for personal attention from a competent and caring staff member.

Once you have adequate resources, the next step is to make sure your staff understand the importance of looking after your existing customers. As we have discussed, there are only three ways to grow a business and keeping existing customers coming back is the easiest and least expensive way. Most managers know this but do their front-line staff? To help your staff understand that your best customer is the one you already have, calculate how much revenue you would lose over the life of the customer if they took their business elsewhere. Then find out how many customers you are losing each year. Multiply these two numbers together and share them with your staff. They will become as concerned as you are about looking after existing customers.

Thirdly, make sure your staff have the necessary product knowledge to be able to help your customers with their purchases. This requires you to provide adequate training to your staff, but it also means building a resource system or database so staff can access information quickly. The bad experiences I had in the two department stores or the restaurant were not the fault of the staff. They were the fault of management who clearly had not bothered to either train staff so they had the knowledge I was looking for, or had not developed information systems that would allow the staff to look up the answers to my questions.

Fourthly, develop processes and procedures for serving customers. Most managers think of processes as being relevant to only manufacturing environments, or IT systems. They think standard operating procedures are necessary only for operating equipment or filling in forms. But there can - and there should be - processes and procedures for such important activities as greeting customers, understanding their needs, presenting options, answering their questions, taking the order, handling complaints and after-sales follow up. Again, the experience I had opening the savings account was not the fault of the employee. She clearly did not understand the value of a new customer nor did she have a process for greeting customers to follow. I once worked with one company that was told by its customers, "We love it when you smile and use our names." Although most people in the company had been involved in getting that feedback and anyone who had not been was told what the customers had said, staff still did not usually smile and use the customer's name. The

Tell your staff the life-time value of your customers.

problem was not fixed until a process was developed for how to greet customers. Even though we know how important first impressions are, most businesses leave how staff will interact with the customer to chance.

All of this adds more expense, you say. That is true. It does cost money to do these things. But think about the increased revenue that will result from customers returning to buy more. Repeat customers cost less to attract, take less time to serve and are less price sensitive. Loyal customers give the chance to enjoy lower costs of sales, higher prices and better margins. It is also possible that this increased level of attention will make your customers feel better about doing business with you, and they might recommend you to others as a result. Again, more sales, lower marketing costs and, of course, people who have already decided to do business with you are going to be prepared to pay a little more for the extra value they have been primed by their associates and friends to perceive they will be getting. It just keeps getting better.

Control and choices

Today's customers want to be in control. One of New Zealand's major banks learned this lesson the hard way recently when they decided to change the savings accounts of 150,000 customers from one where customers earned 1% interest to one where they got only entries into lottery draws. In one issue of the New Zealand Herald alone, there was a small front-page story, a substantial story on Page 2 with a large photo of a very unhappy customer, and an editorial decrying, not only that particular bank, but all banks for being so heavy handed with their customers. The damage done to the goodwill of that bank is incalculable. I personally know of several people who have cancelled their accounts or, worse from the bank's point of view, simply withdrawn their funds and left the account dormant. In every case, they said nothing to the bank. They made no complaints. They just voted with their feet.

To give people control, you have to be prepared to be customer driven. That means that you have to be willing to change the way you run your business so that it works for your customers, not just for you. Today's customers want to shop when it suits them, not when it suits the shopkeeper. Businesses want to do business in a way that suits their business, not in a way that works for their supplier. People want to be in control and they want to have choices. These have to be real choices, not just illusions. Recently, I spoke at a conference where we had a formal banquet. Before the meal was served, the caterer announced that they had two choices of entree, salmon or pasta. The serving staff then came around and alternated the entrees. One person got salmon, the next got pasta, then salmon, then pasta. They had a choice of entrees all right - and they made the choice for you! Admittedly, one of the staff did announce that if anyone had a dish in front of them which they did not like, they could get up and find someone to trade with!

You cannot sell what you do not have

Giving customers choices means having a range of products and services from which customers can choose. This is difficult to do in a small country like New Zealand, but nevertheless it is important to our customers. Many retailers would do well to learn this lesson. I am amazed at the number of times I go into a shop to buy something I have seen advertised only to be told that they do not have it in my size or in the colour I want. "We can get it in from another of our shops, or you could go to one of our other stores," I am often told.

"No, thank you," I say. "You have just learned the first rule of retailing. You cannot sell what you do not have."

Once I was told, "Yes, we can. People just wait." I left the store wondering what planet he lived on.

Having choices and being in control are very important human needs and customers will pay a little more to do business with companies who allow them to control the transaction. Do market research to find out the different ways that your customers would like to be able to do business with you and allow them to make choices based on their preferences. To make this happen, you will need to have flexibility in your processes and staff who understand that at the end of the day, the customer is the boss.

Products and services in the Bronze Zone are worth more to customers than naked solutions in the Commodity Zone. Wrap your naked solution with reliability, speed and convenience, personal attention and information, and choice and control and you will be able to persuade your customers to pay higher prices.

Unless, of course, your competitors have done the same thing. In that case, you will need to create even higher levels of value.

Summary

- A useful starting point to understanding what your customers value is to group benefits into five 'zones.'

- These range from a 'commodity zone' where price is definitely the issue to the 'platinum zone' where price hardly affects the customer's decision to buy.

- If you are providing a naked solution, you are in the Commodity Zone and you will have no choice but to compete on price.

- Reliability, speed and convenience, personal attention and information, and control and choices make up the Bronze Zone. This zone is in your customer's eyes worth more than the Commodity Package.

- If you can wrap that solution with solutions to other problems customers have, you can raise your prices and increase your margins.

- Customers worry about on time delivery, whether something will work or whether their supplier will do what they say they will do. Be reliable and you can charge for it.

- All of us are short of time and energy. Be fast and easy to do business with, and you will find that speed and convenience are worth something to your customers.

- Sometimes we need help and it is useful to have someone there to talk to. Most of us are prepared to pay a little more to do business with someone who is keen to have our business, cares about serving us, and wants our buying experience to be a successful one.

- Customers want to be in control and they want to have choices. This meets a very basic human need.

Think about it

Which of your products and services do your customers view as commodity items?

_____
_____
_____

Could you add more value to your existing products and services by being more reliable, faster or more convenient?

_____
_____
_____

If you are already reliable, fast and convenient, does your pricing reflect that?

_____
_____
_____

Who has control of the way people do business with you? You or your customers?

_____
_____
_____

Do you give people choices?

_____
_____
_____

Do your customers have an AWESOME experience when they shop with you? If not, what needs to be improved?

_____
_____
_____

Chapter 6
The zones of higher value

I love what you do for me.

In this crowded and competitive market full of demanding customers who want everything for free yesterday, customers are looking for increasingly higher levels of value. To be in a position to persuade your customers to pay more, you need to be wrapping your naked solution with more benefits than can be found in the bronze zone.

WHAT CUSTOMERS WILL PAY MORE FOR

GUM THAT COSTS $5 PER STICK, IF IT'S CALLED... 'MADONNA', 'DIET' OR 'PRESTIGE'

A $1000 DRESS MADE OF NEWSPAPER AND MASKING TAPE, IF IT HAS THE RIGHT LABEL

I'LL TAKE IT !!

DINNER FOR TWO THAT COSTS $568, NOT INCLUDING WINE, IF THE MAITRE D' REMEMBERS YOUR NAME

MONSIER DAVID! IT IS A GENUINE PLEASURE TO SEE YOU AGAIN!

The Silver Zone

The Silver Zone goes beyond providing customer service to creating a great experience for your customers, and this great experience begins with the sales process itself. There was a time when selling involved simply showing the customer the value they could obtain from your product or service. Today, when customers have no time and little excess energy, the sales process itself must add value to your customers or they simply will not even look at your offering. Advertisers know, for example, they have only two seconds to convince people browsing through a magazine that they should stop and read their advertisement. How much junk mail do you throw away without even looking at the envelope? The sale call itself must create value whether you are selling business to business or directly to the consumer. In the Silver Zone, the supplier, both through the transaction and the product or service itself, is improving the businessperson's profitability or the consumer's quality of life.

Today, the sales process itself must add value.

Increased functionality

The more your product and service can do for your customers, the more valuable it will seem, providing of course, the things it will do deliver benefits in your customers' eyes and are not just features. If you are to avoid the mistake that most appliance manufacturers have made, the increased functionality of your offering has to make it easier for your customers to solve more of their problems. Automobile manufacturers have done this, for example, by combining the luxury of top sedans with the utility of four wheel-drive vehicles making it possible for drivers to go off road in comfort.

As we have discussed, the key to being able to build more functionality into your product or service is to understand your customers' objectives, and the problems that prevent them from reaching those objectives. Look for ways to allow people to do things they cannot now do, or for ways to make it easier for them to do things.

> "An elite few companies are bucking the trend (to cut prices) by introducing new products that provide benefits people think are worth paying for."
>
> *Alfred Zeien, CEO Gillete*

Back up support

Customers buy products and services to solve problems and to make their lives easier or more enjoyable. Most of us, however, have had experiences as a customer where buying the product or service was when our problems really began! Therefore, many people will pay for features that will provide them with reassurance, peace of mind and a feeling of security. Indeed, the popularity of extended warranties for appliance and cars is a good case in point. Knowing that they can easily return a faulty product or service and get a refund is equally important to customers.

By the same token, people will pay more to buy from a dealer who can give them after-sales service. They want to know that if the product does not work properly, they can have it repaired. They also want to know that if they have trouble using the product or service, they can obtain assistance. These are particularly important when the customer is buying complex or technical products and services, and for most of us is critical when buying computer hardware and software.

All of this may seem obvious to you but the customer's reality is often different. I saw a sign in a well-known chain of bookstores saying that CDs and DVDs could not be returned once purchased. Many computer manufacturers and dealers have after sales service but it is very difficult to use. Even if you do eventually get through to someone on the telephone, you then have to give them a 150 digit authorisation code. I had words with the marketing manager of one company because they had designed a system where a customer could not get through to their 'help desk' directly. They had to leave a message and the help desk staff would call back when it suited them. You would think that if a company made a product or service that did not work properly, they would want to make it very easy for their customer to have it fixed. They would not want their customer sitting around, fuming, while they waited for someone to call them back.

Personal recognition and reward

Recognising your customer and rewarding them for doing business with you goes one step beyond the personal attention provided in the Bronze Zone. Providing personal attention is good customer service but recognising your most valued customers and rewarding them for their business is good customer relationship management (see Chapter 10).

Giving customers personal attention helps them to make the buying decision and to complete the transaction, but recognising them as a valued customer makes them feel good. We all like to be recognised and we would like to be thought of as a valued customer, but most of us realise that we are often only one of a large number of customers our supplier has to deal with. Thus, if we are recognised we begin to experience the 'Wow' factor. Of course, if a customer spends a lot of money with one supplier, or has done business with them over a long period of time, then they do expect to be recognised, and if they are not they will feel very disappointed. My speaking and consulting work takes me to several countries and, as a result, I fly a lot, always with the same airline. Sometimes I can go to the airport several days in a row and there is rarely a long interval between trips. For years it irked me that whenever I walked into the frequent flyer's lounge I had to show my membership card. I learned the names of the staff long before they appeared to recognise me. It did not make me feel my business was very important to them.

We all have egos and we like to be recognised, but even more importantly, we like to be rewarded. Your customers know that you are benefiting from their business and they would like you to show them that you value their custom. That is exactly the feeling your customers would get if you had a reward programme that gave them something extra. The world's airlines are among the best in doing this. Other loyalty programmes such as *Air Miles* and *Fly Buys* allow many other companies to reward their customers for doing business with them. Studies show that customers who belong to loyalty programmes concentrate their spending with one particular supplier within a given industry. One study showed that 53% of people said that the loyalty programme they were in made them less likely to switch and 80% said they spread their business around more before joining the programme. More encouragingly, loyalty programmes appear to encourage people to spend up to 46% more.

Loyalty programmes appear to encourage people to spend up to 46% more.

Thus, customers belonging to a loyalty programme stay with a supplier longer, providing the reward programme remains in place. Loyalty programmes are also a very powerful tool for attracting new customers. But most importantly, customers of companies with loyalty programmes are likely to be less sensitive to the price charged because their perception of the value they receive extends beyond the benefits of the product and service they are purchasing. The benefits of the reward they will ultimately enjoy as a result of being a member of the loyalty programme become part of the value equation in their eyes.

There are two main traps to avoid when designing a loyalty programme. The first trap is developing a reward that no one values very highly. The value of the benefits of a loyalty programme is in the eyes of the beholder. Most of us find that getting a free cup of coffee now and then is not worth the effort of carrying around 50 loyalty cards. Moreover, the value of the free cup of coffee is not worth the cost of going out of your way to get it. In other words, the café loyalty card does not significantly affect purchasing behaviour in most cases. On the other hand, the fact that 1.4 million New Zealanders belong to *Fly Buys*, and that it is growing by 4000 customers a week, demonstrates how highly customers value air travel. The lesson is clear. When you design a loyalty programme, as when you design any product or service, find out what your customers value before you begin.

The second trap that loyalty programmes can fall into is to make it difficult for people to redeem their rewards. Many programmes offering air travel as a reward have come very close to turning customers away from their programmes. If the customer cannot get through on the telephone within their lifetime, if the flights they want are not available while they are young enough to travel, and if the number of points required keeps changing, then the perception of value will diminish significantly.

Special offers

Special offers are a good way to add the increased value necessary to persuade your customers to pay more. As with loyalty schemes, the increased benefits become part of the value equation, increasing the customer's perception of the value being offered. Unlike discounts, which are an expensive way of enticing customers to buy, special offers are inexpensive to produce because they are delivered at a wholesale cost. They are a powerful way of adding value, however, because the benefit is perceived at the retail price. Petrol stations often give away a free bottle of soft drink with purchases over $20, for example. The customer perceives the value of the offer to be a couple of dollars, whereas the cost to the oil company is probably only a few cents.

Fun and entertainment

Every generation in every country in every social class has valued being entertained and having fun. Today's customers are no different. Owning a colour TV within the next two years, for example, is the aim of most families in China. Owning a colour television comes ahead of buying life insurance, kitchen appliances or telecommunications products. In our own society, all cell phones and computers come with games installed and Play Stations, video games and 'pokies' are all big business. Similarly sports cars and convertibles, once thought to be going the way of the dinosaurs are now enjoying a resurgence in popularity and almost every major manufacturer has one either in the market or in production. The vast majority of four-wheel drive vehicles are owned by people who have no practical need for them. These owners are buying fun.

Owners of four-wheel drives and convertibles are paying more for fun.

The National Basketball Association (NBA) in America was having a hard time persuading people to buy tickets at any price not so many years ago. Today, the NBA attracts large numbers of fans who are prepared to pay big prices to attend the games. Things changed when organisers understood there was more money to be made selling entertainment than tickets to sports matches. The huge sums earned by movie stars, musicians and athletes show just how highly we value entertainment.

Health, safety & longevity

There has probably been no time in history when so many people have enjoyed the luxury of being able to improve the quality of their lives.

Oxygen on the rocks

At US$1.19 per litre

By adding herbs such as ginkgo or St. John's wort to their products, beverage bottlers claim to offer healthier refreshments. *Talking Rain Beverage Co.* in Preston, Washington, has another purportedly health enhancing additive: oxygen.

Since early 1998 the company has been bottling an oxygen-enhanced HzO called *Air-water*. It is springwater with more than 10 times the amount of oxygen found in everyday tap water, according to Talking Rain founder John Stevens. To ensure that the air stays in the bottle, *Air-water* is electromagnetically sealed, the company says. Its brochures promote *Air-water* as helping "working muscles to metabolize the needed energy" and giving those who drink it a "second wind."

Stevens, who started the company 14 years ago, concedes that the claimed health benefits aren't well documented. As for taste, he says that the difference between *Air-water* and ordinary water "depends on how much of a water connoisseur you are."

Still, he insists that *Air-water* is "extremely refreshing." A lot of people apparently agree. So far, according to Stevens, Talking Rain has sold 1 million bottles at roughly $1.19 a litre. And it has competition. Several other companies have recently introduced oxygen enhanced drinks with names like *Oxy Squeeze* and *Life 02*.

Thanks to world peace, increased prosperity, more education, mass communication and medical science, a very large number of consumers understand what will enhance their safety, keep them healthy and prolong their lives. In the interests of self-preservation, they will spend money on anything that will help them maintain and improve their health and safety. Indeed, products and services that are perceived as doing that command a premium. Just look at the prices of homoeopathic and naturopathic remedies, dietary supplements and herbal products! Probably no people in the world have free access to thousands of kilometres of golden beaches like Australians do, but a recent study by the University of Queensland found that Australians would be happy to spend A$1.95 to visit popular surfing beaches if the money was used to hire more lifeguards.

The demographics of Western society are such that health and safety will become an increasingly lucrative area of value as baby boomers continue to age. Tens of millions of baby-boomer women, for instance, will be sweating out menopause over the next decade. At least 4900 boomer women start menopause each day in America. Seniors are already a big market with 65% of seniors in North America spending an average of US$10 per week on vitamins. Health related telephone services are used by 46% of seniors. I wonder how much price is an issue for them? If you have a product or service that helps people to remain healthy or safe, you do not have to be a price-taker.

Facts on seniors

*64% spend an average of US$10 per week on vitamins

*46% use health-related telephone services

*52% don't follow a healthy diet because it means sacrificing taste and the food they enjoy

Source: American Demographics, November 1998

New and exciting experiences

One of our basic needs is to experience new things. We crave stimulation and new things are exciting and fun. A new dress, a new car, a new house, a new job, a new holiday destination – we happily spend our money on such things even though we have enough clothes, the present car runs fine and where we went for a holiday last year was just great. The desire for novelty explains why fads such as the hula hoop, pogo stick and pet rocks were so successful. And why they lasted only a limited period of time! People will pay more for something new. Napster is finding, for example, that young people will happily pay on average US$1.05 to download a song if it is a new release. If the song is 18 months old, however, they will pay only than 27 cents.

The growth in popularity of ethnic food is a good example of how people like things that are new and different. This is the age of the ethnic eater where anything exotic will get a place on the customer's menu. Consumers have moved beyond the traditional range of ethnic food, such as French and Chinese dishes, to Caribbean, Middle Eastern foods and also dishes from other Asian countries such as Thailand, Korea and Vietnam. The trend will be towards lesser-known countries such as Argentina, Cuba and Cambodia say industry experts. They also believe restaurateurs will target specific regions, or even regions within regions, and also blend foods together such as Cuban-Chinese, to satisfy the consumer's insatiable appetite for something new.

We need to experience new things.

Novelty stimulates the flow of adrenalin and so does excitement and adventure. Perhaps this explains the popularity of theme parks with rides that take years off your life, and adventure holidays where you pay large sums of money to live in primitive conditions in unhealthy places. Anything you can do to add excitement to your product or service, or to the shopping experience itself will make it easier to persuade your customers to pay more.

Brand or reputation

Many companies have discovered that it is worthwhile investing in

103

developing a brand or reputation that is associated with product or service quality and after-sales support. A known and respected brand makes it easier for customers to make a choice in a market full of complex offerings, and it gives them the peace of mind we just spoke about. Customers, as you probably know from your own shopping experience, will pay for these. If that brand also enhances self-esteem or conveys status then it is worth even more to the customer.

A good example of a company persuading its customers to pay more by branding a commodity product is BP. In 2001, BP introduced Ultimate, a branded petrol that promised better power and more fuel efficiency. Aimed at a niche market, Ultimate sells for 15% more than ordinary unleaded and presently accounts for 5% of BP's total petrol sales. "We identified a niche in the market where the customer is much better informed about fuel," says John McCrindle, BP's retail marketing and development manager in Australia. "These are the people who polish their cars regularly and understand that Ultimate is a better fuel for their engine."

> Go beyond what the customer demands today to keep your customers tomorrow. Understand what consequences (benefits) customers are after and create new and better ways to help customers experience those consequences.
>
> *Quality Progress Magazine*

The Gold Zone

The Gold Zone goes beyond enhancing the quality of life to enriching it to the point people feel pampered. It is the realm of self-indulgence where customers are prepared to pay to have the luxury of specialist advice or to shop in opulent surroundings.

Expertise

Knowledge has always been worth something and that is even truer today. In an increasingly complex world, where customers are overwhelmed by choices, expertise is worth money because the cost of getting it wrong is too high. Imagine getting to 65 and finding that you have been making the wrong investment decisions. Where would that leave you? This is particularly true when selling business to business because if your business customers make the wrong choice it can impact on their ability to satisfy their customers. Because value equals benefits minus cost, whenever you can show your customer that the cost of not using your product or service could be very high, you can command a premium price.

Not only is life complex, it is busy. Many people do not have the time or the energy to deal with matters they know must be handled. We are moving away from being a society of do-it-yourselfers to one where people will pay someone to advise them on what must be done, or even to do it for them. But people must be able to trust these specialists, and that means they must have the skills, knowledge and experience that convince customers they can look after their best interests.

Knowledge is always worth a premium price.

People will pay for expertise. A friend of mine bought an electric organ from somewhere where the price was 'right.' When he got it home, he found he did not understand how to use many of the instrument's features. When he went back to the supplier he found the supplier did not know either. He found another supplier who did know more but they would not help him because he had not purchased the organ from them. If my friend was doing it all over, he would have paid more to get more. How many of us have learned the same lesson the same hard way?

Acquire the expertise people need, show them you have it and how it can assist them and you will be able to persuade your customers to pay more.

Customisation

This is clearly the era of mass customisation. People want to feel special and, therefore, will pay a premium for products and services made just for them. Moreover, things designed with a particular individual in mind often work better too. In a world of 6 billion people, with most of us living in large cities, keeping a unique identity and finding a product or service that works right for us is a constant struggle.

Computer technology has made customisation possible and affordable for many businesses. Body scanning devices, for example, have been developed and are in use in some stores in Europe and Japan. These devices can map out 300,000 points on the body and produce 48 video snapshots. This information can be used to custom manufacture clothing for the customer.

> From theme funerals to theme weddings, from customized charm bracelets to design-it-yourself shoes, consumers are seeking services and products with a personal touch. In fact, 85% of 18-24 year olds wish more products and services were customized according to a July study from American Demographics and Harris Interactive.
>
> *Entrepreneur*

Another good example of how mass customisation can be used to create value is the London-based fund management company group called Mercury Asset Management which is owned by the Merrill Lynch Group. Mercury recently released a mass-customised magazine called The Mercury Investor's Guide. The 46 page publication comes out twice a year with personalised pages in 7700 versions! To develop the magazine, Mercury first identified its most valuable customers and then segmented them into 22 groups. It then interviewed customers in each segment to find out what differentiated them. Telephone and postal surveys were carried out to get a better understanding of each customer's holdings and needs. Mercury then used the information to customise the publication. In addition to a personalised greeting, content is tailored to the client's age and portfolio of assets. The response from customers was amazing. In the first three weeks, the customised guide attracted 141% more business than the previous guide did in four weeks. By contrast, Mercury sent a generic version to 5% of its customers in each of the 22 segments and no new business was generated as a result.

Ambience

Most of us would like to be pampered. If only we could afford to be! Fortunately, an increasingly large number of us can. Products and services once considered to be luxuries available only to the rich have now become affordable to middle-class consumers. Nearly all luxury car manufacturers, for instance, have developed models within middle-class budgets. Although these products are more affordable, they still command a price premium.

Consumers like to live the good life, if only for a few hours. Restaurants that become places of entertainment, bookstores that are like coffee shops, and coffee shops that are like living rooms, are all able to persuade their customers to pay more. Look at how Starbucks has transformed a functional product into an emotional one. Coffee and coffee shops used to be a commodity product. The only way companies knew how to compete was on price. Then Starbucks came along and created what customers often call a 'caffeine induced oasis' offering a chic gathering place, relaxation and exotic drinks.

The appeal of luxury and comfort is just as relevant when selling business to business. In the travel industry, for example, the trend in Europe is towards a clear split between business and leisure travel. Major airlines, departing from major airports are increasing the number of business class seats in their aircraft to such an extent that some experts predict that within a year all weekday flights out of the major airports will be business class. Imagine the impact that a plane full of passengers paying business class fares will have on the bottom-line! Leisure travel will be left to low-cost budget airlines - in reality offshoots of the major airlines - which have a different value proposition for their customers. But you can see what will happen, can't you? When all leisure travel is low cost and low benefit, some company will come along and will differentiate itself by offering increased luxury, at an increased price of course.

Most of us would like to be pampered.

> "Think of things you would like to have someone do for you, all the dirty jobs. There's enormous potential here for entrepreneurs with imagination."
>
> Arnold Brown, American trend analyst

Enhancing self esteem

Feeling good about yourself is a basic human need and therefore any product or service that fills that need will command a premium price. One example of this is the huge personal growth industry. Another is the health centre or fitness business which seems to me to be as much about shaping the body as developing physical fitness. But perhaps the best example is the cosmetics industry which is today almost as big for men as it is for women. More than 80% of the cost of producing these products comes from packaging and advertising as companies position their products as ways to enhance self esteem through glamour and prestige.

> "In the factories we make cosmetics. In the shops we sell hope."
>
> Charles Revson, founder of Revlon

Organic and natural

People seem to attach even more value to products which are organically grown or natural. Such products appear to be perceived as going beyond the health products in the Silver Zone. There is a belief that organically or naturally produced products cost more to produce. There is also a view that in this synthetic world, anything natural has got to be better.

Innovation

In today's crowded marketplace innovation is very important to business success because people will pay for something that is new, better or bigger. Innovation requires large amounts of time and money but the return often justifies the investment. Gillette, for example, invested large sums of money to develop the *Mach 3* razor but since it was launched it has had a great response from customers - and sells for 50% more than its predecessor. Similarly, Colgate developed a new toothpaste called *Colgate Total*, which is the first toothpaste to be approved by the US Food & Drug Administration as a remedy for gingivitis. Colgate Total sells for 25% more than conventional toothpaste and is now the number 1 brand. Toyota developed Lexus and within three years it accounted for nearly one-third of the company's operating profit although Lexus sales were only 2% of Toyota's unit volume. Sony created the *Walkman* in 1979 and since then it has made the greatest contribution to Sony's profitable growth.

> How do you make things worse for a strong brand like *Tide*? Cutting prices won't work; *Tide* will only match them. Advertise more? *Tide* will just outspend you. There's only one way to blow a box of *Tide* off the shelf: come out with something bigger, better and newer.
>
> *Fortune Magazine*

The war for market share between Proctor & Gamble and Unilever, two of the major players in the fabric-care market, is being fought and won on innovation. Proctor & Gamble's *Tide* has 40% market share and its sales have climbed 41% over the past five years principally because the company has developed a relentless stream of new and improved products. Innovation is particularly important in the grocery business where the main battle is for shelf space. Launching a new product is a great way to win space at the expense of your competitors. "When something new comes in, something else has got to go out," says Susan Chachil, a category manager for Kmart.

Social causes

Both experience and research are showing that people will pay more to buy from companies that support social causes. This is a relatively recent phenomenon and goes beyond being a good corporate citizen or doing business ethically. Clearly customers feel good being associated with an organisation that is making a contribution to society. Is this driven by a sense of guilt or obligation from the customer? Or, is it simply that customers believe that companies that give something back deserve their business? Whatever the reason, adopting a social cause to support is good for business. Anita Roddick found that with the Body Shop (no testing of cosmetics on animals), similarly McDonald's (Ronald McDonald's House for the parents of children in hospital) and in New Zealand, WestpacTrust with their helicopter or the ASB Bank with their community trust.

This particular benefit is easy to deliver. All you need is a large enough margin to be able to donate money without it affecting your return on investment and enough marketing dollars to tell the world about the contribution you are making to society.

The Platinum Zone

This is the pinnacle of the value hierarchy and, therefore, accessible to only a small niche. It goes beyond the feeling good of the Silver Zone or even the indulgence of the Gold Zone.

Status and prestige

Status is one level beyond self-esteem. Status is more than someone feeling good about themselves. It is when their worth is recognised by others. All people should expect to have good self-esteem but only a relative few have status.

Every society has levels of status. The American Declaration of Independence may state that all men are created equal, but most of us enjoy being treated a little more equally than the next person. Many people strive for status and are therefore prepared to pay more for products and services that might give them that. How else could you explain branded clothing? Shops are full of clothes with fashionable labels which are sold for twice the price although they do not look any better or do any more for you than clothing without the brand labels.

Kiwis say we care

A landmark study just released, *Good is gold - the Stillwater/AC Nielsen Report*, shows New Zealand consumers and employees consistently support good causes and are reaping the benefits in their brand and reputation.

The research surveyed 1,000 New Zealanders and marketing directors from some of New Zealand's largest companies, and looked into consumer awareness and attitudes towards companies that integrate support of worthy causes.

Cause-related marketing is a strategic positioning and marketing discipline which links a company and its products to a social cause or issue. It is different from philanthropy.

The survey found that 85% of New Zealanders tend to think more highly of a company that supports charities while 94% feel that it is a good idea for New Zealand companies to take this position. 74% of respondents said they would change their normal brand if a similar brand supported a cause they believed in, depending on if the price was equal, but **65% said they would even pay more money to support a worthy cause.**

The Main Report

Status is important in the area of business to business as well. One of the best examples comes from the computer chip-maker Intel. They were so successful in building a status brand that computer manufacturers proudly display a sticker on the outside of their machines saying 'Intel inside'. Once upon a time Xerox could command a premium for the status its brand conveyed, as could IBM.

Scarcity

The laws of supply and demand mean that anything that is in short supply will be valued. Airlines understand this very well and, thanks to computer technology, have been able to develop very complex pricing models where the price increases as demand soars and availability shrinks. The Coca-Cola Company also recognises this and as I said earlier, in 1999 the company experimented with a vending machine where the price of a Coke rose as the temperature increased. The next step is probably a machine that X-rays your pocket to find out how much money you have and then sets the price accordingly!

The laws of supply and demand mean that anything that is in short supply will be valued.

No one understands the value of scarcity better than collectors – or those who sell to collectors! Suppliers of rare books, stamps, coins, paintings, and antique furniture know they can obtain a premium for these products because the ravages of time have diminished the available supply. But many companies have learned that by producing something in limited quantities they can create scarceness immediately. This has even extended to personalised license plates. It makes no sense that the license plate 'A1' should be worth any more than 'M2', but then again most buying decisions are emotional.

The value of scarcity lies in the prestige of owning something very unique. Unlike our other cousins in the animal kingdom, we are not happy being one of the herd. If you own something that is recognised as being rare, and therefore is highly valued, you will set yourself apart from the madding crowd. And to some people, that is worth a lot of money.

Summary

- If you want to persuade your customers to pay more, you will have to provide more value. It is useful to think of three zones of higher value.

- The Silver Zone goes beyond providing good customer service to creating a good experience for your customers.

- Building increased functionality into your products, providing back up support, giving personal recognition and reward, making special offers, providing fun and entertainment, contributing to your customers' health, safety and longevity, providing new experiences and having a strong brand are all components of the Silver Zone.

- The Gold Zone goes beyond enhancing the quality of life to enriching it to the point people feel pampered.

- Having high levels of expertise, customising your product or service for each customer, creating an environment with ambience and luxury, enhancing your customer's self-esteem, offering organically grown or naturally produced products, innovating to offer products and services that are unique, and supporting social causes are all components of the Gold Zone.

- The pinnacle of the value hierarchy is the Platinum Zone.

- Benefits in the Platinum Zone include helping your customers to achieve high status or prestige, and offering products and services that are unique and scarce.

Think about it

Which zone of value is each of your products and services in?

What could you add to each of your offerings to move them into the next zone of value?

What new products or services could you develop that would be in a higher zone of value than where you currently operate?

How much more could you earn from your products and services if you could move each one to a higher zone of value?

# Chapter 7
Persuading your customers to pay more

Selling is turning value into cash.

It was not a good day for Bill Roberts. As regional sales manager for a large corporate, he was under constant pressure to achieve the ambitious sales targets set by Head Office. Yesterday that target had been increased yet again, and he suspected the increase was necessary to pay for a large cost over-run caused by someone else in marketing. To make matters worse, today one of his best sales people handed in his notice, saying he would be gone in two weeks. Desperate to have people out there selling, Bill thought about whom he could get as a replacement. One of the first people to spring to mind was Tricia Culvert, a young woman who had joined the company only a few months earlier. Tricia was working in administration and, as far as Bill knew, she did not have any sales experience but that did not put him off. She's bright and has excellent people skills, he thought to himself, and he set off to talk to her.

Bill found Tricia at her desk surrounded by tall piles of papers. "Tricia, let me take you away from all this!" he said.

"Why, Bill. I didn't know you cared," she blushed.

"No, I mean, how would you like to leave all this behind and have a career in selling?"

"Right now, that sounds very appealing, Bill," she said laughing. "The problem is, I know nothing about selling."

"That's not a problem," said Bill. "Selling is very easy. It will take you no time to learn how to sell."

"I'm not sure I believe that. I see how hard you and your team work. And, I know how much trouble you have meeting your targets!" she added, her eyes twinkling.

115

"Tell you what," said Bill, "I'll show you just how easy it is. We'll go for a walk down the street. You pick a building and we'll walk in. You choose a person and I'll sell them my watch. I bet you I can get them to take it within two minutes of talking to them."

"You're on, Bill. This I've got to see."

They walked down the street and Tricia suggested they go into the first office building they came to. On the ground floor there was a receptionist sitting at a long counter, and behind her were a few desks with people working.

"See that man with the grey hair," said Tricia pointing to a man sitting at one of the desks, "Let me see you sell your watch to him."

Bill approached the counter. "Can I help you, sir?" the receptionist asked.

"I'd like to speak to that gentlemen over there," said Bill pointing to the man Tricia had chosen. "Could I speak to him for a minute, please?"

The receptionist went over to the desk and whispered something to the man. He glanced at Bill once or twice while she talked to him and looked puzzled. Nevertheless, he came to the counter.

"Can I help you?" he asked uncertainly.

"Sir, I would like to sell you my watch," said Bill, slipping his watch off his wrist and holding it out for the man to see. "It is very good and keeps excellent time. Would you like to buy it?"

"Err, I don't think so," the man stammered. "You see I can't really afford a new..."

"You don't understand, Sir," said Bill interrupting him. "The watch is free. And this is not a joke. I am the owner of this watch. It runs very well. Indeed, it's nearly new. I would like you to have it for nothing."

The man hesitated for a few moments. "Well, alright," he said. "I'll call your bluff." And he reached out and took the watch. "Thank you very much."

Bill turned away smiling and walked out of the building with a flabbergasted Tricia trailing behind. Outside he stopped and before she could say a word, he said: "See, selling something is easy. The trick is getting a good price for it!"

In today's competitive world, many salespeople are on the defensive. Their response to having to fight for sales in a crowded market place full of hungry competitors and very demanding customers is to sharpen their pencils and discount their prices. What they have forgotten is that getting a good price for their products and services is *their* job. Bill was right. Any fool can give something away. And, many do!

If you are in sales, getting a good price for your products and services is your job!

Successful salespeople, on the other hand, are on the offensive. They know their first job is to help build so much value into their company's products and services that their customers are comfortable with the prices being charged; prices that allow their company to make a good profit. Salespeople should play a key role in creating value because

The trick is learning how to get a good price for it!

they are the eyes and ears of the company. They are constantly talking to customers and therefore, armed with the right questions, they can help their company learn about their customers businesses, the problems they face, and what it would be worth to them to have those problems solved. They should pass this information on to those within the company who are responsible for product design, pricing and marketing. Secondly, successful salespeople sell on value not on price. These salespeople know their customers will ask, "Why should I pay more?" They are prepared for this question because they understand that it is their job to provide the answer.

Salespeople are the eyes and ears of the company.

Successful salespeople make their presentations in such a way that their customers are happy to pay the asking price because they can see what the benefits of the products and services are worth to them. Imagine, for example, that your financial adviser telephones you one day and says, "An insurance company has just come out with a really good product. If you become ill with a life-threatening disease such as cancer, or if you have a heart attack or a stroke, they will pay you a lump sum benefit of $100,000. This coverage costs only $720 each year. Can I come and talk to you about it?"

Which part of that conversation are you thinking about right now? Probably the price. You are most likely wondering whether you want to fork out another $720 a year to one more insurance company? Now that is a no-brainer if ever there was one!

Imagine instead that your adviser telephones and says: "If you were diagnosed with a life-threatening illness such as cancer, or if you had a heart attack or stroke, what problems would you have?" Imagine, too, that after you have listed a few problems, the adviser goes on to ask, "If you were given $100,000 at that time, would it help you to deal with those problems?" You would probably answer, yes. After all, most of us would find $100,000 useful no matter what the circumstances.

"Well," says your adviser, "I could organise for you to receive $100,000 in the event you were stricken with a life-threatening illness and it would cost you only $60 per month for that facility. Are you interested?"

Which part of the conversation are you focused on this time? I bet you are still thinking about the problems you would have if you became seriously ill. You might even have progressed to contemplating how you would spend the $100,000 if disaster struck, but I doubt that you are thinking much about the price of the product.

It is the old story; we should sell the sizzle and not the steak. Most of us have heard that saying but most of us are still selling the steak. In today's health conscious world, for example, grocery stores are full of fat free and low fat products. Most of these carry such names as 'Lite This' or 'Lite That' because the manufacturers are selling features not benefits. It is a fool who sells on the basis of features because customers only ever buy benefits. One company that understands this is Talley's Frozen Foods in Motueka. They call their frozen dairy dessert, *Guilt Free*. Now that is selling the benefit!

To sell the value, you must understand the problems that your customers have, and what they would gain if you could solve those problems for them. This is made easier, as we discussed in Chapter 4, if you are selling what your customers are buying. You will remember, that your customers are buying enhanced profitability if you are selling business to business, or enhanced quality of life if you are selling directly to consumers. The conversation you have with your customers should then be aligned with what they are trying to buy. I once asked the manufacturer of agricultural chemicals to demonstrate for me the conversation they would have with their customers, who were re-sellers. "Mr Shopkeeper," they role-played, "you should buy this new product of ours because it will kill 50% more weeds than any competing product. It lasts longer and therefore is more cost effective..."

Sell the sizzle and not the steak.

"Is that the conversation you should be having with the shopkeeper," I asked, interrupting their presentation, "or is that the conversation the shopkeeper should be having with the farmer?" I told them I thought the problem with their sales presentation is that while they were talking about killing weeds, shopkeepers would be asking themselves how much they would have to invest, what the return on that investment would be, how long the stock might sit on the shelves, what marketing support they would get and whether they could return unsold stock. "Your customers are thinking dollars and cents," I told them, "and you are talking about weeds. No wonder the first thing your customers say when you have finished talking is, 'What discount will you give me?'"

You should be talking about how you will improve the consumer's lifestyle or enhance the businessperson's profitability.

The conversation these salespeople should have been having with their customers was about how their product could have enhanced their customers' profitability. That is likely to be the issue that your customers are interested in when you are selling business to business. I was once on the receiving end of a sales presentation from someone who understood that and it was most impressive. I was chairman of a small confectionery business that manufactured hand-made chocolate products. We sold wholesale and we also had a retail outlet ourselves. One day when I was in the shop, the managing director told me he wanted to install a fudge-making system. That seemed like a good idea to me since fudge would complement the range of chocolate products we had in the store. I asked him what the system would cost.

"Ten thousand dollars," he replied.

"Wow, " I said, surprised at the cost. "Where are you going to put it?" I was thinking that it had to be pretty big for that amount of money.

"I thought we could put it on this little table," he said.

I told him he was crazy to even think about paying so much for something that would sit on a little table but he convinced me that we should at least meet with the salesman and hear his story. I agreed and two weeks later we met the salesman for lunch.

"Would you like to increase your revenue in your store by 33%?" he asked as soon as we had sat down.

Selling the sizzle

Plumber: "We repair what your husband fixed."

Tyre shop: "Invite us to your next blow-out."

Plastic surgeon: "We'll pick your nose!"

Muffler shop: "No appointment necessary. We'll hear you coming."

Bowling alley: "So quiet you can hear a pin drop."

Counsellor: "Growing old is mandatory. Growing wise is optional."

Undertaker: "Drive carefully. We can wait."

Optometrist: "If you can't see what you're looking for, you've come to the right place."

Psychic: "Don't call us, we'll call you."

Podiatrist: "Time wounds all heels."

Electrician: "We'll remove your shorts."

Taxidermist: "We really know our stuff."

Towing company: "We don't charge an arm and a leg. We want tows."

"I'll bite," I said.

"Right," he said, taking out a binder crammed full of photos in vinyl sleeves. "First, you buy a display cabinet that looks like this," he told us, showing us his first photograph. "You don't want one that looks like this," he said, pointing to another picture, "or like this." It's got to look like this one here and he explained why. "Now, draw me a floor plan of your shop." We did as we had been told. "Right, you put the cabinet here," he said pointing to a side wall. "You don't want it here or here. It's got to be there." Again, he explained why.

"Now, you make between seven and nine different flavours of fudge," he told us. "You don't make fewer than seven because you want to give people a choice and you don't want to make more because you will confuse them. When people come into the shop you do not ask them if they would like to taste some fudge, you ask them which flavour they would like to try." For ninety minutes he told us how to sell fudge. Not once did he talk about the features of his fudge system.

Needless to say we bought the system. Here was a salesman who understood that it would be a difficult task to convince people to pay $10,000 for a small fudge-making system, but a relatively easy sale if he could show people how a small investment of $10,000 could increase their revenue by a third. Yes, we did get the increase he promised. In fact, we increased our revenue by over 35% because we charged more than the $27 a kilo he said we should. "You can't charge $30 a kilo for fudge," he told us one day, amazed at our stupidity.

"People don't buy a kilo of fudge," we replied. "We sell it in 100 gram lots just like you told us. They might not pay $30 for a kilo, but they will pay $3 per 100 grams." And we were right. They did.

Another key to selling on value is to know the problems your customers have - or could have if they did not have your product or service. Then you must make your customers aware of how much these problems are costing them, or could cost them. Unless you do this, your customers will question the price because they will see only the cost of purchasing, not the cost of not purchasing.

People often forget that there are no free lunches. I once talked to a fellow who was trying to sell a $15,000 water pump to the owner of a boutique freezing works that killed deer on contract. The owner was renowned for having short arms and deep pockets so the salesman was not surprised when he rejected the offer to purchase a new pump. I asked the salesman why he thought there was a need for a new pump. "Because the staff say the water pressure is too low," he told me. I asked why that was a problem. "Because it takes longer to clean up.

With low water pressure, it takes longer to hose things down," he said. I asked why anyone should care about that. "Because that is time that could be spent killing deer," he said. I asked how many. "Well, the guys on the floor say that it takes 10 minutes longer to clean up, and according to government regulations there must be three clean-ups a day, so that is half an hour in lost production. They could process 6 deer in that time." I asked how much they earned from each deer. "About $200," he said.

"So let's see if I understand this," I said. "The owner could buy the pump for $15,000 or he could lose $1200 per day in lost production. Is that right?"

"I think I know what I need to talk to the owner about," he laughed.

The same principle applies even if there is no problem at the moment, but there could be in the future. I once got some quotes on a house-load of timber. I asked one supplier why his prices were higher than the others. "Well, there are some people out there who are pretty good at passing off Grade B timber as Grade A," he said. "I guarantee mine is all Grade A." I began to think of what problems I might have if we had structural problems later on because we bought inferior timber. Then I thought about the cost of remedying those structural problems and all of a sudden this fellow's quote looked like good value.

If it is that easy to persuade customers to pay more, why do so many salespeople, even experienced ones, sell on price and not on value? I think one of the reasons is that most of us have the wrong view of selling. I say this because three years ago I had the honour to speak at the Million Dollar Round Table, the world's largest convention of financial advisers and life insurance agents. It was a magnificent affair, held in New Orleans, with over 8000 of the world's top agents in attendance. These were the cream of the crop because every year agents have to qualify to attend this conference and the standards are very high.

We have the wrong view about selling.

During the five days of dynamic speakers, stimulating workshops and magnificent entertainment, I began to sense that there was a hidden

Sell the value by asking questions

You can make a powerful sales presentation simply by asking questions that lead the customer to appreciate the benefits that your product or service can offer them:

- "What is the biggest problem facing your company right now?"
- "Why is that a problem for you?"
- "How much is that problem costing you?"
- "What solutions have you tried already?"
- "How did they work out?"
- "Based on your experience, what do you believe would have to happen for that problem to disappear?"
- "If we could do that, how would it help you?"
- "What would it be worth to you to have that problem solved?"
- "What would you save or gain if you did not have that problem?"
- "What are you doing to handle that problem now? How much is that costing you?"
- "Do you have problems using the product or service you are now using? What is that costing you?"
- "How often do you have to replace the product you are using now?"
- "What does your existing warranty cover?"
- "If we could deliver faster than anyone else, would that save you money?"
- "If we could make it easier for you to get a solution, would that save you any money?"
- "Would our solution help you to satisfy your customers more? How would that benefit your business?"

agenda. It seemed to me that one of the key objectives of the conference, which is organised by agents not by insurance companies, was for these agents to convince themselves that selling life insurance was a good thing to do. This surprised me for two reasons. First, these agents were top achievers, so why would they be having a crisis of confidence? Secondly life insurance, especially term-life, is truly a miracle product. After all, there are not many things you will buy in this world where, you or someone you nominate is guaranteed to receive at sometime in the future more than was ever paid for the product. So again, why the self doubts?

5 Steps to value-based selling

1. **Understand** that you are giving your customers a chance to improve their lifestyle or the profitability of their business and that that is worth a lot to them *in their* eyes, not just yours.

2. **Focus** your prospective customer's attention on what they are trying to achieve (improved lifestyle or enhanced profitability) and on the problems which prevent them from doing that.

3. **Help** your customers to calculate what those problems are costing them - or could be costing them.

4. **Help** your customers to understand how your offering's benefits can *make them money*, and how the reduced non-financial costs can *save them money*.

5. **Show** them how the gain from the benefits *plus* the savings from the reduced non-financial costs is less than the price of your product or service.

I began to think that even these experienced and successful salespeople had the wrong view of selling. It seemed as if most salespeople believe that selling is persuading customers to do something they do not want to do. Perhaps, before making a sales call, they think to themselves that their customers will not *really* want to spend their hard earned money purchasing the products or services they are selling? Thus, they expect they will be dealing with an unwilling buyer who will have innumerable objections to purchasing what they are selling. But this is the wrong view of selling!

Selling is giving people the opportunity to buy solutions to problems that bother them.

Selling is not persuading people to do something they do not want to do. It is giving people the opportunity to buy solutions to problems that bother them so much they are willing to part with their hard earned money to get them. Just think about your own behaviour. How often do you struggle to find a parking space and battle with crowds just so you can give someone else your money? How often have you been disappointed because you could not buy what you were looking for? How many times have you trooped all over town trying to locate something you needed? You would have been happy to pay for any of these things – if only you could have found them. It is the same for your customers.

You have a choice

You do have a choice. You can sell on price or you can sell on value. But you need to understand that if you do not sell on value, you must sell on price. You must also understand that selling on price, as we saw in Chapter 1, is dangerous. But most importantly, there is no need to sell on price. It is an issue but rarely *the* issue. Therefore, value-based selling makes the most sense.

The key to value based selling is to make your solution so attractive that your customers would be upset if they could not buy it. Is your value proposition clear? Can your customers readily see how the benefits outweigh the costs? Is your pricing simple and easy to understand? Have you provided a detailed explanation of the prices you charge relating pricing to value (both increased benefits and reduced costs)? That is how you get your customers to buy without having to discount. That is how you get your customers to pay more. Learn to do that and you will never have to compete on price again.

10 Powerful words that sell the value

Fast: Time is the most precious commodity for people today.

Guaranteed: This takes the risk out of buying.

Simple and easy: This takes the effort out of using the product or service.

Limited: Scarce means valuable to most people.

Free: Everyone likes to think they are getting a bargain.

You and Your: If it is personal to you, it is worth more to you.

Important: If it is important, it must be valuable!

New: New is fresh, exciting, leading edge.

Improved: If it is better, it must be worth more than the old one.

Luxury: People like to think they are pampering themselves.

Get the incentives right

Sales people are critical to your success in achieving better margins because they carry your value message to your customers. If they understand the value of a product or service to the customer, if they understand the importance of achieving the best price, and if they have the motivation to work to achieve that price, you will be able to persuade

Don't be afraid to charge more Even in tough times.

When I interview customers to find out why they buy from a particular supplier, they frequently mention salesperson confidence as a decisive factor in the purchasing decision.

Why should confidence be so critically important in an economic downturn?

There's a widespread fallacy that in hard times customers buy on price. Nothing could be further from the truth. In hard times customers buy safety. In studying IBM's customer base during the last recession I discovered that, for computer hardware at least, customers actually paid 12 percent more on average for equivalent equipment than they did in easier economic times. Why? First, in hard times decisions are more likely to be made by committees, and lower-risk options are generally favoured in group decision making. Generally, the lower-risk option carries a higher price tag. Second, buyers realized that their decisions would come under more scrutiny and they would personally be blamed if equipment didn't perform. The old slogan, "nobody ever got fired for choosing IBM" was a potent selling tool, even if it meant a price premium.

So what's the bottom-line advice for selling in hard times? Focus on the best opportunities, and don't chase everything that moves. Invest in strategy, planning, and preparation. Be confident. Sell the safety and reliability of your offerings and don't think that you have to compete on price.

Come to think of it, that's not bad advice for selling in good times either.

Neil Rackham, author of SPIN Selling *and, more recently,* Rethinking the Sales Force.

your customers to pay more. But you must have them working with you. Your sales team, along with their managers must understand that large numbers of sales or market share does not necessarily equal profitability.

Persuading your customers to pay more, then, begins with persuading your sales people that their job is to contribute to the company's overall profitability, not just to make a sale. To do that you need to have your targets and incentives aligned with the key profit driver, which is usually margin not volume. The danger is that most sales incentives put the sales person's interests in conflict with those of the company. In commission selling, for example, a 5% reduction in price will have the effect of decreasing the sales person's income by 5% but for the company that 5% reduction in price could result in a loss on that transaction. Where the sales person might take the view that 95% of something is better than 100% of nothing, the business owner might prefer not to have the sale at all.

Incentives for a given transaction should be related to margin achieved or, better yet, overall profitability. Incentives should also be related to customer retention so that your sales people do not spend all their time prospecting for new business, ignoring valuable existing customers in the process. When they are prospecting, make sure your sales people are rewarded for bringing in the kinds of customers you want to do business with. If incentives are related to margins, profitability, customer retention and acquiring the right kind of customers, you can be sure your salespeople are being driven by the same critical success factors as the rest of your company.

Summary

- Getting a good price for your product or service *is your job*.
- Successful salespeople help their company create more value.
- Successful salespeople sell on the basis of value not price.
- Understand that selling is not persuading people to do something they do not want to do; it is giving them the opportunity to buy solutions to problems that bother them.
- Sell the sizzle, not the steak.
- Show how your offerings will improve the consumer's lifestyle or enhance the businessperson's profit.
- Understand the problems your customers have and what it costs them to have those problems.
- Show your customers there are no free lunches.
- Help consumers to understand how the benefits from your products and services are worth money to them, and how the reduced non-financial costs can save them money.
- Help your business customers to understand how the benefits of your product or service can make them money, and how the reduced non-financial costs can save them money.
- Show your customers how the gain from the benefits plus the savings from the reduced non-financial costs is less than the price of your product or service.
- Reward your salespeople on profit from sales or overall company profitability.

Think about it

Are your salespeople persuading you to lower your prices or your customers to pay more?

How much information do you or your salespeople feed to head office to help build more value into your company's products and services?

What would you have to do differently to be able to pass on more information?

Are you or your salespeople selling on price or value?

When you sell on price, what does it cost you?

Are you or your salespeople selling the sizzle or the steak?

How could you sell the sizzle more effectively?

Which of the 5 steps to value-based selling could you do more effectively?

How could you increase your effectiveness?

Are you rewarding your salespeople for the right behaviours?

Chapter 8
Handling price objections

An objection is something to be handled, not a reason to lower the price.

Of course your customers will talk about price. After all, as the story about the electricity company shows, we have spent years teaching our customers that price is the main issue. But in spite of our teachings, price is not the main issue. Value is. Your customers do not want lower prices; they want better value. Specifically, they want to increase their own profits, if they are business customers; or to improve the quality of their lives, if they are consumers. It is true that your customers believe, usually mistakenly, that buying the cheapest product or service will help them get better value, but as you know from your own personal experience, the lowest price does not always equal the best value. The trick in handling objections to price, therefore, is to remind your customers of this lesson.

Nevertheless, your customers will object to your prices. Accept it, and like a good boy scout, be prepared for it! They will ask themselves, and probably also you, "Why should I pay more?" As we have discussed, it is your job to have an answer to that question. Here are some strategies for handling price objections that, in my experience, work very well.

Remind your customers that the lowest price does not always equal the best value.

Raise the issue first

Prevention is always better than cure. Therefore, one of the most effective ways to deal with the issue of price is to raise it yourself before your prospect does. There are five advantages to raising the issue of price yourself. First, it allows you to manage your customer's expectations. You might say, for example, "This is not the cheapest car

133

> "It's unwise to pay too much, but it's worse to pay too little. When you pay too much, you lose a little money, that's all. When you pay too little, you sometimes lose everything because the thing you bought was incapable of doing the thing it was bought to do.
>
> The common law of business balance prohibits paying a little and getting a lot-it can't be done. If you deal with the lowest bidder, it is well to add something for the risk you run. And if you do that, you will have enough to pay for something better."
>
> *John Ruskin*

on the market ... ." This statement creates in the customer's mind the expectation that price is not the main issue and that they will be paying more, but for good reason. Secondly, by raising the issue of price before your prospect does, you are showing that you have confidence in both the value your product or service delivers and the price you have put on that value. This sends a strong signal that says, "There is no point arguing about the price here. We know what our offering is worth." Thirdly, raising the price early in the discussion is a way of qualifying the purchaser and will allow people who are looking for the cheapest car in the market to opt out, thereby saving both their time and yours. Many salespeople are reluctant to do this because they do not want to do anything to jeopardise a sale. These people need to be reminded that the objective is not to make a sale. It is to make a profitable sale.

Raise the issue of price before the prospect does.

The fourth advantage in raising the issue of price early is that at this point price is not *the* issue. There are many things the customer is interested in learning about. Price is just one of them. As a result, raising the price in your sales pitch allows you to go on and sell the value. Thus, you might say, "This is not the cheapest car on the market, but it is one of the safest and most reliable vehicles you will find." Because your customer wants to learn about the value your product or service can deliver to them, they will be open to hearing what you have to say. This will not be the case later on when they are trying to beat down the price. At that stage, anything you say will be seen as an attempt to counter their move to get you to lower the price. Rather than listen to you, they will be thinking of how to refute what you are saying.

The fifth and biggest advantage in raising the issue of price in the early stage of the sales presentation is that it gets it out of the way early. In most cases, while you are talking to the customer about the benefits of your product or service, they are saying to themselves, "Yeah, but what's it going to cost me?" This means you do not have 100% of their attention. If they are not fully hearing what you are saying, what is the point of saying it? To make matters worse, you *know* they are doing this, and so while you are making your presentation, you are thinking, "In a minute they are going to ask me about the price and when I tell them, they will complain that it is too high. How will I deal with that?" Therefore, you do not have 100% of your attention! How effective is your presentation likely to be if you are only partially thinking about what you are saying and they are only partially listening?

Put the price issue to rest early on. Show them you have confidence that the price you are charging reflects the value they will get from what you are offering. Show them you are not embarrassed about the price, and that you are not afraid of discussing it.

Believe in your offering

Two years ago, I was approached by a company to give a keynote address at their annual conference. A senior manager interviewed me and he seemed keen to have me speak. He explained, however, that the final decision was the chief executive's and that I would be hearing from him soon. The next week the CEO sent a fax confirming they would like me to address their conference. "The trouble is," he said, "my board of directors is quite tight-fisted so would you please look at reducing your fee."

Now I admit, there was a time when I would have automatically discounted my price in the face of such customer pressure but those days, thankfully, are gone. I sent the fax back with one question scribbled across the bottom: "Do your people deserve the best?" Within an hour he faxed back saying they accepted my original price. This experience obviously had some impact on him because when I did speak at the conference several months later, the CEO introduced me by telling his staff what I had done. He then suggested that they do the same thing the next time one of their prospects tries to beat down the price.

Know the value of your offering and believe in it.

Your product or service *must* be delivering value to your customers otherwise no one would ever buy it. That value is worth something. Know what it is and believe in it. Accept that many people will object to your price just to see if you will yield. Be prepared for this. When they do raise price objections, look them in the eye and say, "We know this is what this offering is worth to people. If you would like to obtain the value that is built into our product or service, this is the price you will have to pay." Remember, when you lower the price, you are diminishing the worth of your own skills and effort, and those of your company's, too. As I recall, even Karl Marx agreed that a person is worthy of their labour.

Demonstrate that price is not THE issue

I was running a seminar on pricing and I could see that one of the participants was growing increasingly impatient. Finally, she could contain herself no longer. "This is all very good," she blurted out, "but what do you do when your customers complain about the price?"

Another of the participants smiled. "I'll tell you what I do," he said, his eyes twinkling. "When my customers complain about the price, especially when they say they could buy what I'm selling cheaper elsewhere, I stop the sales pitch and start to pack up my stuff. 'You're probably right,' I tell them. Then I turn and look at something they are wearing. 'Say, that's a nice tie you have on,' I say.

"They usually look pleased with themselves and say something like: 'Oh, do you like it? I bought it at such and such a store.'

"I then tell them that I suppose they bought the cheapest tie in the store. They usually look offended at hearing this and reply, 'As a matter of fact, it wasn't.'

"I ask them, 'If it wasn't the cheapest, why did you buy it?' They usually tell me they bought it because of the quality, or its appearance or such like. Then I pick something else they are wearing and repeat the process. After I have gone through everything I can see them wearing, it becomes clear to both of us that they rarely buy something because it is the lowest priced. I then ask them, 'If you don't buy the lowest price clothes why would you buy the lowest price widgets? Your clothes have little impact on your business success but the value of the products and services you buy can have a huge impact.'

"That takes care of most price objections," he laughed.

He had a very good point. As we discussed in Chapter 2, one of the biggest myths in business is that price is *the* issue. Most of us, although we value our money, do not base our buying decision on price, or price alone. If you help your customers to realise that, it will cause them to re-evaluate their response to your offer.

Your prospect is probably not wearing anything they bought solely on price.

Understand what they are saying

What does it mean when people say, "It is too expensive," or, "Your price is too high?" We assume, of course, they are complaining about the price but in reality they might be saying, "I accept that your offering is worth that much but I cannot afford it." Or perhaps they are really saying, "I could afford it but if I bought it right now, I would have trouble managing my cash flow."

An objection about the price can mean a great number of things, and many of them have got nothing to do with money. In another life, I was a clinical psychologist in private practice. I always found that the first session with a new client was the most challenging. I had to get to know the client and form a relationship with them. Then I had to learn about their life, their problems, why they came to my clinic and what they hoped to achieve. I also had to form a diagnosis and a treatment plan, and then sell it to the client. And I had one hour to do all that!

How much money are they willing to spend?

Customers frequently say they can only spend a specific amount of money, when in reality they might be willing to spend more for the right deal. How can you confirm this? Say something like, "I understand you're prepared to spend up to $100, but if I were to show you something for $200 that operates as well as our $500 item, would you be interested?" The response will let you know how serious the price limit is.

The Main Report

One of the issues I had to discuss with clients at the end of the first visit, of course, was my fee. I had to convince people who were generally feeling overwhelmed and hopeless, that it was worth spending their hard earned money (there was no insurance coverage) to obtain my services. Occasionally someone would say they could not afford my fee. My usual response was to say, "I understand, and because I think it is so important that you get some help, I will see you for nothing."

Almost always the person would reply: "Thank you, but I guess it's not really the money. The whole thing seems so scary. I'm afraid of what I might discover if I start looking into myself." The barrier to buying was not price. It was fear. Price was the handy excuse.

HANDLING PRICE OBJECTIONS

In the business world, when people complain about the price, they are often saying: "I do not see the value here." According to informal polls I take with my audiences, most people in the Western world have very strong negative feelings about the fees their banks charge them and, indeed, believe they are being unfairly charged. They have this view because, as we discussed in Chapter 4, they do not see the value in the fees they are being charged. Every month, these customers review their bank statements and moan about charges such as the 25 cent cheque

Bank customers do not see the value behind the fees they are being charged.

Listen to your customers. They will tell you everything you need to know to persuade them to pay more.

handling fee, the $3 cash handling fee, the $30 activity fee for keeping an account open. But what they do not seem to complain about is the $1234.79 interest payment on their mortgage, or their $345.26 dollar car payment. Why? Because they understand that if they did not pay $1234.79 each month they would not be able to live in their lovely house. In other words, they know the value of these costs. The same cannot be said of the myriad of other monthly fees their bank charges them. One bank actually wanted to change this so they asked me how they could sell the value their fees represented. I told them the first thing they had to do was identify the value. They set to work doing this. Then they came back to me and said, "We have found two fees for which we cannot see any value. How do we sell those?"

When your customers do complain about the price, do not assume that it is the price they are complaining about. Ask questions and listen carefully to the answers to understand what the real issue is. When you do, you will be able to find a way to deal with that issue. But first, you must understand it. Time spent listening to your customers is never time wasted because your customers will tell you everything you need to know to be successful in persuading our customers to pay more.

Help your customers to be successful

Many customers worry about price because they know that they will have to justify the purchase and the purchase price to their own boss or group to whom they are accountable. Consequently, while you are talking to them about the value of your offering, they are visualising their boss saying to them, "Why did you pay so much for these widgets? We could have bought them much cheaper from ACME." They can also see themselves having no good reason to support their decision for having paid the price you are asking. Since no one wants to look foolish in the eyes of their boss, they will attempt to get the price reduced.

Give your customer the ammunition they need to prove they bought well.

You could try to convince your customer that the price is fair and reasonable, but since that is not really the issue, you are not likely to be successful. An alternative is to give your customer the ammunition they need to convince their boss that they bought well. This is best done in writing. Prepare a 'fact sheet' outlining how the benefits of your products and services outweigh the costs of purchasing them, and why it is prudent to spend that little bit more, getting these benefits. Then go through this information with your customer and leave them a copy of the fact sheet so they have the ammunition they need to look good in the eyes of their boss. This approach will work best if you think of your customer's boss as being your customer's customer. Find out all you can about what this person is trying to achieve and which obstacles lie in their path. Find out what they value and what is on their shopping list, just as you would with a prospective customer. Then use this information to show your customer how they can make their boss successful.

Stress the costs of not buying

As we saw in Chapter 7, there are no free lunches. For every benefit you receive, you pay a price, but when it comes to buying things, people often forget that. It is your job to remind them.

Be they businesspeople or consumers, people invest a great deal of time, effort and emotion trying to accomplish something. As a result, the purchase price is often the least expensive cost they pay. Reminding your customers of this can help you persuade them to pay more. For example, look at the very clever advertisement for a trout-fishing leader called the *Umpqua Deceiver Leader*, used in fly-fishing. Clearly the *Umpqua Deceiver Leader* costs more than your average run of the mill leader so Feather Merchants, the distributors of this product, employed Mike Stent, one of New Zealand's most experienced trout fishermen, to handle any price objections. In the advertisement, reproduced below, Stent is quoted as saying, "It's silly not to spend that little bit extra on your leader or tipper to give yourself the extra chance that your trout can't see your leader in a small clear river like the Tauranga-Taupo."

Is it worth saving a few cents?

Now, put yourself in the shoes of a prospective customer. You like to fish for trout with a fly rod, and you are in a fishing store thinking about

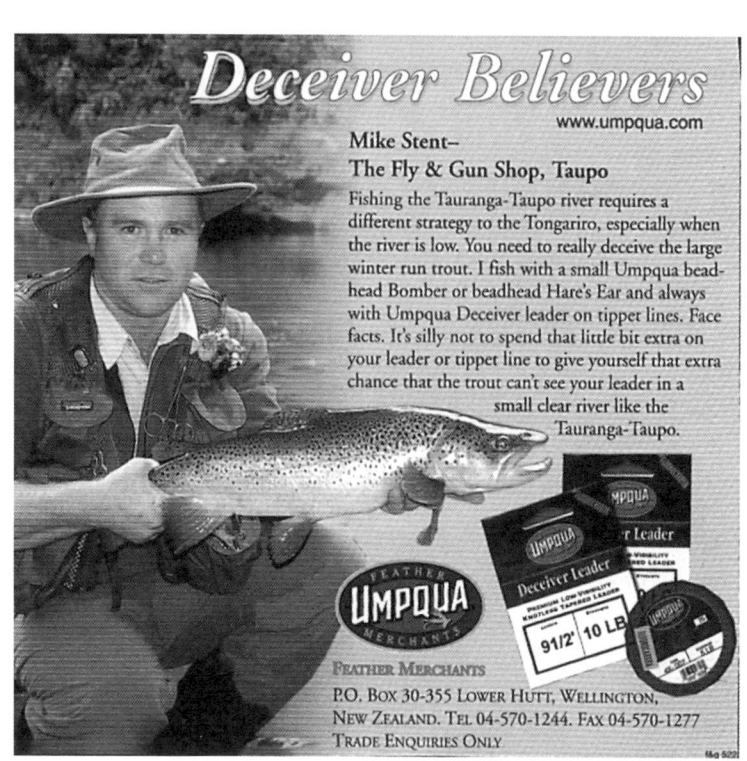

Reproduced with permission from Feather Merchants

buying a leader. Will you buy the cheapest? You might think about the money saved and say 'yes.' But you are much more likely to think to yourself, "I will get up in the dark and cold at 5 a.m. I will drive down a rough track and then walk through the bush to a likely looking trout pool. Then I will wade into the freezing water and stand for several hours in the strong current with water up to my chest, making cast after cast, hoping to attract a wary trout. As I stand in the water, which will matter more – that I saved a couple of dollars or that I hooked on to the big one?" If it takes you any time to think about this, you have never been fly-fishing!

Understand what your prospective customer is trying to do. What are the risks? Where could they lose out? What would it cost them in either money or non-financial costs, if the product or service let them down. How do these costs compare with the purchase price? This alone should make it possible for you to handle price objections. Once, when I was undertaking some major house renovations, I asked a timber merchant why the prices he had quoted me were a little higher than some other suppliers. "There are some people out there who are pretty

A supplier's poor performance could cause your customer grief.

Do they want to take that risk to save a few dollars?

good with a can of spray paint," he told me. When I asked him what he meant by that, he explained that some low-cost suppliers were selling Grade B timber as Grade A and that was why their prices were lower. I started to think about what problems I would have if I used sub-standard timber, and what it would cost to solve those problems. All of a sudden, the few dollars to be saved did not look like a good bargain. This way of dealing with price objections should be very useful when selling business to business because the potential cost of things going wrong for businesspeople is huge. If their suppliers let them down, they will end up disappointing their customers and that, in turn, could be disastrous for their business.

Remember, this IS your job.

Your customers will raise objections to your price because we have done such a good job of convincing them that price is the main issue. It is your job to handle these objections, and the first step to doing that is to be prepared. Tell yourself that, firstly, your customers would contest the price no matter what it was and, secondly, it is your job as a sales person to deal with that objection. Then prepare for the sales call by gathering some information about your customer's business.

Any idiot can draw a line through a number and write a smaller number underneath, and many do!

What are your customer's customers demanding from them? How can your product or service help them satisfy their customers? Find out who the 'customers' of your customer are. In other words, to whom do they have to justify the decision to purchase and the price paid? Once you know this, give your customer the ammunition they need to prove they made the right decision when they bought from you at the price you asked. When your customer does object to the price, do not cave in. Remember, any idiot can draw a line through a number and write a smaller number underneath, and many do! Show them that the cost of paying a fair price is usually less than the cost of getting a bargain. There are, after all, no free lunches.

Summary

- Your customers will object to price so be prepared for it.
- One of your best strategies is to raise the issue yourself before your customer does.
- Have confidence in the value of your offering. Defend its value.
- Demonstrate that price is not the issue when they buy things for themselves, so why should it be when they are buying for the business or the family?
- Understand what your customers are really saying when they complain about price.
- Help your customers to be successful. Give them the ammunition they need to demonstrate that they bought well.
- There are no free lunches. Stress the cost of not buying your product or service.
- Do not cave in under the pressure to discount. Getting a good price is your job.

Think about it

Which objections do your customers raise about the prices you charge?

Develop a strategy for responding to each one.

Chapter 9
How to profit from your relationships

"Human relationships are declining in the selling game."
Jack Welch, former Chairman and CEO of General Electric

Achieving the full profit potential from each customer relationship should be one of your key goals. To do this you need to understand the size of each key customer's wallet. In other words, how much money are they prepared to spend over a year on the products and services that you and your competitors offer. Secondly, you need to know what proportion of that money you are likely to get; that is to say your 'share of their wallet'. Thirdly, you must build a relationship with your key customers and then use that relationship to persuade your customers to spend a greater share of their wallet with you.

You can increase your share of your customer's total spend in four ways. You can persuade them to:

1. pay higher prices.

2. buy greater quantities of the products and services they already buy.

3. buy some of your other products and services.

4. stay with you longer so that over a long period of time they do all of the above.

Make your relationships work.

The best way to persuade your customers to give you a greater share of their wallet is to build a relationship with them. The trouble is, your customers do not want a relationship with you. They are probably having enough trouble with all the other relationships in their lives to have the time and energy to develop a relationship with you! What they do want, however, is to get their needs met and their problems solved. If developing a relationship with you helps them do that, then they will happily respond to your overtures. Just remember, in your customer's eyes, the relationship is not the end but the means. They do not want the relationship, they want to get their needs met. If having a relationship with you means you understand their needs better, if it makes it easier and faster for them to get what they want, if they get additional value from being recognised as a valuable customer, then the time and effort they put into developing a relationship will be worth while. If you want your customers to value their relationship with you, then they must believe they are getting more benefits from that relationship than they are paying in costs.

> Some of the very things we are doing to build relationships with customers are often the things that are destroying those relationships. Too often we are skimming over the fundamentals of relationship building in our rush to cash in on the potential rewards of creating close connections with our customers.
>
> *The Harvard Business Review*

The relationship should be the means to the end for you too. You will invest a great deal of time and effort in building relationships with your key customers and you should make sure you get a return on that investment. You can benefit from your investment by using these relationships to learn more about your customers. You want to learn what you would have to do to persuade them to pay higher prices, or to increase the number of products and services they buy, or to persuade them to purchase your other products and services. In my experience, companies do not do this. I can think of several suppliers who have

Use your relationships to learn:

- What your customers value.
- What their dreams, goals and objectives are.
- What obstacles lie in their path.
- How their business runs.
- What it would be worth to them to solve those problems.
- What problems they have doing business with you.
- Who their key customers are.
- What is important to their customers.
- What problems they have satisfying their customers.
- Where you will be allowed to make a profit.
- How much they spend with you and your competitors.
- How you differ from your competitors in their eyes.
- Why they buy from you.
- What they would miss if your company disappeared.
- What you do for them that no one else does.
- What no one is doing for them.
- How much more business you could do with them.
- What you would have to do to get that business.
- What you do that does not interest them.
- What you do that annoys them.
- Who likes you in the company and who does not.
- How they like to interact with you.
- What would make life easier for them.
- What the opportunities to on-sell, up-sell and cross-sell are.
- Which customers you really want to keep.
- Which companies you should not be doing business with.
- How often to call on your key customers.

CRM delivery gap

A first of its kind report commissioned by the Direct Marketing Association, Microsoft New Zealand, Ceritas Digital and Pivotal Corporation provides an in-depth look at the state of the customer relationship management (CRM) industry in New Zealand.

Key findings from the report suggest that businesses are not maximising the advantages available from best practice CRM. A gap analysis between uptake of CRM and subsequent effectiveness shows high disparities.

For example, of the 262 managers who responded to the survey, 82 percent said they had implemented a CRM strategy to retain customers, but only 51 percent believed the process was fully delivering on its promise. Others felt there was plenty of room for improvement. Similarly, when it came to improved sales and marketing efficiency (a key goal for 79 percent of managers surveyed) only 41 percent of managers believed their CRM strategy was being fulfilled - a gap of 38 percent.

worked hard to build relationships with me. Clearly I benefit from these relationships and because I do, my suppliers have the benefit of my ongoing business. However, they are not using their relationships with me to learn more about me; about what I value; about what they would have to do to get more of my money. What a waste!

Even those companies that practice customer relationship management (CRM) do not take full advantage of the opportunities that having good customer relationships offer. Instead of using their relationships to get close to their customers, they use them to push their customers into behaving in ways that suits their business. Banks are particularly prone to doing this. I have frequently heard personal bankers say, "We need to relationship manage that customer." They are talking about managing the customer through a relationship instead of managing the relationship with the customer so that both parties benefit.

Many studies are showing that companies are not getting the benefits they expected to get from their investments in CRM. Perhaps this is why. There is no point in embarking on CRM unless you are prepared to put your customer at the centre of your universe, invest in learning as much as you can about them, and then use this information to change the way you run your business. In other words, there is little point investing in CRM unless you are prepared to become customer driven.

Make customer retention No 1.

The customer you will most easily build a relationship with, and who you will most easily persuade to give you a greater share of their wallet, is the customer you already have. Customers who know you and who have had a good experience buying from you in the past will be much less price sensitive and much more willing to increase the number of purchases they make. This is especially true for customers who believe that you are an important part of their own success. These customers will think of you as their partner and if they do, price is not likely to be a significant factor in their buying decision.

Unfortunately, most companies do not leverage their relationships with their existing customers because they pay more attention to attracting new customers. This makes little sense because tomorrow's profits will most easily come from yesterday's customers returning to buy more goods and services at higher prices. Not only is there a high opportunity cost from not looking after existing customers, there is a high direct cost. It will have taken money to attract and sell to that customer in the first place, and if a company does not use its relationship to retain that customer, they will have wasted a lot of that investment. This could involve a lot of money since research suggests businesses typically lose 50% of their customers every 5 years.

The customer you will most easily persuade to pay more is the customer you already have.

What is the life-time value of your key customers?

1. Think of one of your valuable customer groups.

2. Now think of how much a typical customer in that group spends each month.

3. Multiply that figure by 12 to get their annual spend.

4. Now multiple the annual spend by 15 to get the life-time value.

5. How many people like them might this customer influence to purchase from you?

6. How much might each of them spend a year?

7. Multiple that figure by 15 and then multiply that figure by the number of people you estimate your customer might influence to buy from you.

8. Is it worth investing time and money building a relationship with that original customer?

Most companies have no idea of how much they are squandering however, since very few know exactly how many of their customers defect each year or how much business they take with them. According to a recent study by KPMG of 2000 Australian and 1000 New Zealand companies, 66% of CEOs said that retaining their most profitable customers was their most important marketing objective, yet 72% could not identify customers at risk of defecting, 70% did not know their annual rate of customer churn, and 45% said they had no idea why their customers left. Of those who did know their rate of churn, 10% said they lost 20% of their customers every year.

The results from KPMG study lead the researchers to conclude that most CEOs do not understand the concept of the lifetime value of a customer. As a result, they do not understand what loyal customers are worth to them, and therefore they do not understand the cost of customer churn, or what it costs them when they lose customers. When senior managers in these companies do calculate what customer churn is costing them, customer retention quickly becomes their Number 1 strategy!

There is a lot to be gained from getting customers to stay longer. Some studies indicate that if a company reduced its defect rate by 5%, it could double its profits. Other studies suggest that reducing customer churn by 2% would have the same effect on your bottom-line as cutting costs by 10%.

Use your relationship to create a GREAT experience

One of the great myths in business is that satisfied customers are loyal customers. This is simply not true. A wide range of studies shows that anywhere up to 85% of the customers who defect were happy at the time of defecting. To retain your customers, they must be very satisfied. To be very satisfied, they must have a great experience when they deal with you. Amazon.com, for example, creates a human relationship with its customers even though it is an e-supplier. It knows what books you have bought in the past and is able to use that information to suggest other books you would like to read. It can provide reviews on books you are interested in that are written by people just like you. As a result, customers love Amazon, even though it does not offer the lowest prices. They love it because the shopping experience has been carefully crafted so that customers actually enjoy it.

If you have close relationships with your customers, you can use those relationships to learn what it would take to give them the kind of experience that will keep them coming back for more. Blockbuster Videos, for example, discovered that between 14% and 20% of customers walked out of their stores dissatisfied because they could not get the video they wanted. Realizing this was unacceptable, Blockbuster studied the rental history of customer segments and used this information to develop a computer programme to predict specific customer demand for a new release. As a result, Blockbuster is able to guarantee the availability of key new titles in most markets. This has enhanced both customer satisfaction and loyalty.

Use your relationship to sell more

The second most effective strategy to grow a business is to sell more to existing customers. This strategy, often called the penetration strategy, involves on-selling, up-selling and cross-selling to increase the amount of money a customer spends with you. Again, if you have a good relationship with a customer, you can use this relationship to learn what you need to know to be able to do this.

Totally satisfied customers buy more

> Xerox has found that its "totally satisfied" customers are 6 times more likely to re-purchase Xerox products during the following 18 months than its "merely satisfied customers" were. Although "totally satisfied" ranked only two points higher on their satisfaction scale than "merely satisfied", it earned six times more loyalty.

I experienced a good example of this a few months ago when my VCR died. My wife and I decided to shop around for a replacement and our first stop was at Harvey Norman. As soon as we entered the store we were confronted by an overwhelming array of VCRs. As we stood there, dazzled by the range of choices, we were approached by a young salesman who asked if he could help. We told him we wanted to see some VCRs and explained our requirements. After listening to what we had to say, he asked a couple of questions. Then he took us directly to a VCR and said, "Based on what you have told me, this is the machine for you." He then explained why it was the right machine.

Both of us were impressed with his approach and satisfied with his recommendation. It was the first store we had been to, however, so we told him that we wanted to shop around before making a purchase. A few quick visits to other stores confirmed our view that Harvey Norman was the place to shop so back we went. We found our helpful salesman and said we wanted to buy the machine he showed us. He collected the machine and walked us over to the cash register. As he was processing the transaction, he asked why we were buying a new VCR. I told him that our old machine had just given up the ghost. "This machine comes with a one year warranty," he told us, "but you could have that extended to five years," and he mentioned what that would cost. Since he was a friendly and helpful sort of fellow (in other words, since he had done such a good job of building a relationship with us), I asked him what he thought. He said that since the other machine had died, it would probably be a good idea to have the longer warranty period. Because he had a relationship with us, we trusted him and spent the extra $75.

Again, because we had a relationship with this salesman and therefore trusted him, I asked if I was likely to have any trouble tuning the new VCR to my TV set. He said that he didn't think so. "But I have Sky Digital," I said. "Will that make it any harder?"

"Probably not," he replied. "But if you are concerned about it, we could get Tisco's to do it for you. It would cost only $30," he told us, "and they could

We are delighted to have spent $105 more.

do it tomorrow. In fact, you wouldn't even need to carry the new VCR home. They will come and collect it here on the way to your place." That, of course, is what we did. Because this salesman took the time to build a relationship with us, and because he used that relationship to understand our needs, he was able to persuade us to spend $105 more than we had intended. And we were delighted to have done that!

Not all customers are the same

Not all customers are the same and therefore should not be treated in the same way. Today, nearly everyone in business understands that and therefore most companies are attempting to segment their

> ### How are your customer relations?
> - How do you refer to your customers when they are not around to hear you?
> - Do you speak up when you hear your colleagues complaining about customers?
> - In your heart, do you believe that having customers is a privilege?
> - Would your colleagues and customers agree with your answer?

customers into different groups. Unfortunately, most seem to do this only on the basis of what the customer spends with them. Thus, A customers are those who spend the most and D customers are those who spend very little. This is a very crude model of segmentation and is fraught with problems. For example, this model looks at what customers are currently spending with a company, not what they could potentially spend. Since the model is used to determine the resources that are invested in a particular customer group, it can be a self-fulfilling prophecy. Because they are only D customers, the business does not invest in building a relationship with these customers, which means they do not feel particularly strongly about the company, so they spend their money elsewhere and remain D customers.

There are better, more sophisticated ways of segmenting customers. The first step to persuading customers to pay more is to create superior value, and the first step to doing that is to understand what your customers value. In other words, you need to know what they are prepared to pay for. You need to understand what problems they have and what they would be prepared to pay to have those problems solved. Using demographics can be helpful, for example, because demographically based customer segments may help you to understand what your customers value. Young, single, professionals, for instance, may have lots of disposable money but little time and therefore will pay for convenience and speed. Using psychographics is an even more useful approach to segmenting customers because psychological characteristics are even closer to describing value than demographic ones.

An even better way is to segment your customers according to their relationship with you. For example, you will have customers who are **transactional customers or mercenaries**. These customers are primarily focused on price and constantly seek the lowest price supplier. They are expensive to service and they show no loyalty. There is also little or no potential to grow your business with them. These are the customers who spring to mind when you think of putting your prices up. Fortunately not all of your customers will fall into this category. Nevertheless, most companies who look at the profitability of their customers are horrified to find how many fall into this category.

Do not treat your customers as if they were all the same.

Another category is **niche customers**. These are moderately profitable customers but they take only one or two of your products or services, and consequently they are likely to view you as only one of a cluster of suppliers. They expect good service but are still price sensitive. They do have potential for future growth, however.

A third category is **major use customers**. These customers see you as being a major supplier and are either reliant on one of your products or services or buy a wide range of your products or services. They are usually highly profitable customers with potential for developing the relationship further. Major use customers demand a preferential level of service and expect that you will go out of your way to help them. They also expect to be consulted about new products and services that you may be considering developing.

A fourth category is **strategic partners**, and without doubt these are your most valuable customers. That is to say, if you have any strategic partners - because most companies do not. These customers are already highly profitable and have great potential for increased profits for both you and them. Strategic partners expect you to be proactive in discussing your long-term goals and strategies with them. They also expect you will be prepared to talk about how you can link your strategy with theirs so that both parties can achieve their long-term objectives. Strategic partners expect you will work with them to develop new products and services that are exclusive to them. They are even happy to merge business processes.

Two other categories of customers companies have are hostages and terrorist- defectors. **Hostages** are customers who have to deal with you whether they want to or not. This is because you have a monopoly or near monopoly position, or because they are part of a large organisation where the purchasing decision is made elsewhere and then forced on the rest of the organisation. Hostages feel resentful and often bitter because they have lost the power of choice. Therefore, when dealing with hostage customers it is important to work twice as hard to create value as you would if they did have a choice. The objective is to create so much value that your hostage customers say to themselves, "Even if I had a choice, I would want to do business with this company."

Terrorist-defectors, of course, is a segment of customers you would rather not have. Yet every company can expect to have some customers who fall into this category. It is important that you know who these customers are and build a relationship with them so that you can understand what it is you are doing that is driving some customers away. Like all terrorists, this group can do a tremendous amount of damage to you in your home marketplace. Perhaps if you had a relationship with them you could minimize, or even neutralize, the harm they could do.

Segment according to value

Since your customers do not want your products and services, but rather the value they can extract from them, I believe the best way to segment customers is according to what they value. If you can do this, you will find it a lot easier to target your products and services, and also your marketing activities. If you know that people value being pampered and you can design an offer that will pamper them to death, you will find it easy to persuade them to pay more. Similarly, if health and longevity is their concern, organically produced foods and natural health remedies will be what they want. And as you know from your own experience, such products are usually available only at a premium price.

The American fast food company, Taco Bell, took this approach and identified two groups of customers: penny pinchers and speed freaks. As you would imagine, penny pinchers were concerned about price, and on average bought only three to four products which were all at the lower end of the price range. Speed freaks on the other hand, were more concerned about getting their meals quickly, and therefore tended to buy higher priced items from Taco Bell's menu. Taco Bell was surprised to find that these two customer groups accounted for 70% of the company's volume although they represented only 30% of the total customer base. Armed with this information, Taco Bell reoriented its business to cater to these two customer segments. They redefined their business concept, repositioned the entire organisation and re-engineered its core processes just to be able to give penny pinchers and speed freaks what they wanted. Sales increased from US$1.6 billion in 1988 to US$4.5 billion in 1994. Profits increased from US$82 million to US$273 million over the same period.

Not many companies have reached this level of sophistication in segmenting their customers. If you can build customer segments around what people value, and if you can use this information to customise both your offerings and your marketing activity, you will find it easier to persuade your customers to pay more.

Develop a strategy for each segment

However you segment your customers, you should remember that the object of the segmentation exercise is to be in a position to treat customers in different segments differently. Transactional customers who cost you money, for example, should be fired. Then you should find ways to rip out the cost of servicing those transactional customers who are marginally profitable. Niche customers should be the target of up-selling and cross-selling campaigns as you try to get them to use a wider range of your products and services. The way to do this is to

---

Who are your key customers?

(And what do you know about them?)
- List them by name or by group.
- Where do they live?
- What jobs do they have?
- What is their income?
- Which hobbies and interests do they have?
- Which cars do they like to drive?
- What do they watch on TV?
- Which books, magazines and newspapers do they read?
- How do they spend their disposable income?
- What do they do in their spare time?
- What are their dreams?
- What are their fears?
- Who makes the buying decisions in the family?
- How do they arrive at that decision?

understand their business better and to show them how you can solve a wider range of their business problems. The emphasis with major use customers should be to turn them into strategic partners. Work to grow the relationship to the point you develop a single strategy aimed at increasing profits for both of you, and by merging business processes. Strategic partners are already your most important customers and this is where a great proportion of your resources should be devoted. They will be the least price sensitive of any of your customers and the least likely to defect. Work to strengthen the relationship by taking over parts of their non-core business, developing exclusive products and services and joint marketing (for example, *Intel inside*).

Relationships are your roads to success

The objective in business is to have profitable customers who stay with you for a long period of time. Therefore, your strategy should be to focus on doing more business with your best customers rather than trying to be all things to all people. The key to doing this is to build strong relationships with your key customers and then to use those relationships to better understand them. You particularly want to understand what they value. That is to say, you want to know what each customer segment is prepared to pay for. When you do, use this knowledge to develop offerings that are targeted to various segments and use it to differentiate the way you interact with each segment.

Your relationships with your customers are truly the roads to your success. They are the routes to being able to persuade your customers to pay more. As we saw from my experience buying a new VCR, even in the area of fast moving consumer goods it is possible to build a *Aim to do more business with your best customers.* relationship and use it to generate higher value sales. Therefore, relationships with customers are worth building properly. Get them on a solid foundation and remove all the rough spots. Then invest in maintaining these relationships so they give you trouble free travelling as you journey towards business success.

Summary

- Achieving the full profit potential from each customer relationship should be your goal.

- Make your relationships work for both of you.

- The relationship should make it easier for your customers to get what they want and possible for you to learn all about your customer.

- Your first priority should be to use your customer relationship to retain your customer's business.

- Make sure that both you and your staff understand the lifetime value of your key customers.

- Use your relationship to create a great experience for your customers by understanding how they want to interact with you.

- Remember that 'very' or 'totally' satisfied customers are much more likely to repurchase than those who are merely 'satisfied.'

- Use your relationship to sell more. Learn what is important to your customers and what problems they are trying to solve and use this information to on-sell, up-sell and cross-sell.

- Remember that not all customers are the same so they should not be treated in the same way.

- Segment your customers. A good approach to segmenting your customers is to group them on the basis of their relationship with you. An even better approach is to group them according to what they value.

- Have a unique strategy for each customer segment. Develop product and service offerings that are tailored to the needs of each segment and also customize the way you interact with each segment.

- Relationships are your road to success. Therefore it is worth investing the time and money in building super highways that will lead you to business success.

Think about it

How could you make your customer relationships work better for your customers?

How could you make better use of them to learn about your customers?

How much does customer churn cost you each year?

How could you look after your existing customers better?

What opportunities to on-sell, up-sell and cross-sell are you not taking full advantage of?

How do you segment your customers? Could you do this better?

What is your strategy for dealing with each segment?

Chapter 10
Your next steps

"If you can dream it, you can do it. Always remember, this whole thing was started by a mouse."
Walt Disney

Call a meeting of all your staff, or at least those who have contact with your customers.

Make a list of the things you know your customers value. Remember, value is what you have that your customers want so badly they are prepared to pay for it. What do you know about your customers' shopping list, their value hierarchy? These are things you know for sure, not things you believe. They will be problems that bother them so much they are prepared to give you their hard earned money to have them solved.

Next make a list of the actions you could take to learn more about what your customers value. What problems to they have that you are not addressing? What do you do that makes it difficult for your customers to do business with you? What problems do they have satisfying and keeping their customers? Ask your customers. Observe your customers. Talk to your customers' customers. Learn more about your customers' businesses, their goals, their dreams, and the obstacles that lie in their path. The more you learn about your customers' problems, the more opportunities you will find to create value. The more value you create, the easier it is to persuade your customers to pay more. Decide who is going to do what by when. And then do it!

The more value you create, the easier it is to persuade your customers to pay more.

Find out how much your customers value these things. In other words, how much are they prepared to pay to have their problems solved, or to get what you have that they want? Write down what you do know. But if you are like most companies you will not know a great deal about how much your customers are prepared to pay, not with any certainty at least. What are these problems costing them? What would they gain if these problems were solved? What would it be worth to them to have these problems fixed quickly, conveniently and reliably? Make a list of actions you could take to learn the answers to these questions. Again, decide who is going to do what by when, and then do it.

> Untapped value is often hidden in complementary products and services. The key is to define the total solution buyers seek when they choose a product or service. A simple way to do so is to think about what happens before, during and after your product is used. Babysitting and parking the car are needed before going to the movies. Operating and application software are used along with computer hardware, In the airline industry, ground transportation is used after the flight but is clearly part of what the customer needs to travel from one place to another.

Later, when you have done more fieldwork, hold another meeting. Use the information you have learned to improve your existing offerings and to create new products and services. **Also, use this information to sell the value you have created.** Remind your sales staff that persuading your customers to pay more is their job. Develop sales techniques to explain to your customers how they will be dollars ahead if they buy your product or service at the price you have put on it. Be able to show them how much they will pay if they do not buy. In other words, show

Remind your sales staff that persuading your customers to pay more is their job.

them what the problem is costing them right now, or what a potential problem could cost them. Finally, identify ways to demonstrate what your customers would be saving because you are fast, easy to do business with and reliable. Develop a script your sales people can use to go through this with your customers. Rehearse the script through role-plays. This not only gives your salespeople the chance to practice the script, when they each play the customer, it gives them the opportunity to see the world through the customers eyes.

Finally, prepare for the price objections you know you will get. Anticipate them, and develop a response for each of them. Again, script it to make it easier for your sales people to use. Rehearse it through role-plays.

This is not something you do just once, of course. It needs to be done continually. You need to create a culture within your organization where people understand that the objective in business is to have profitable customers who stay with us for a long period of time. You do not want unprofitable customers, and once you have profitable customers, you want to keep them. You want staff to be constantly asking themselves, "What would have to happen for our customers to happily pay more."

Never forget, however, that there is a link between your performance and your customer's acceptance of your price. It is essential that your company delivers what you promise to deliver. You must get the basics right. If your staff do not have sufficient product knowledge, or if you are out of stock, not delivering on time, making mistakes with invoices, or letting your customers down in other ways, there is little point trying to persuade them to pay more. Fix your performance problems first.

The objective in business is to have profitable customers who stay with you for a long period of time.

A final word

Like so many things in business, persuading your customers to pay more is like a riddle. There is always an answer to a riddle, but it is not usually obvious. In fact, you have to engage in some lateral thinking to discover it. There is always an answer to the question, "What would have to happen for my customers to happily pay more?" It is not always apparent, but it is always there.

I hope this book has given you some tools and clues you can use to solve the riddle of how to persuade your customers to pay more. Just keep reminding yourself, and your staff, that:

- Price is not the issue.
- It is possible to persuade your customers to pay more.
- It is their job to do this.
- It will significantly improve your profitability if they do.

I would like to end our time together by giving you some practice in riddle-solving.

Riddle:

Three frogs were sitting on a log. One decided to jump off. How many frogs were left on the log?

Answer:

Three frogs were left. Deciding is not the same as doing.

Moral:

Do not decide to increase your profits by persuading your customers to pay more.

Do it!

About the author
Dr. Ian Brooks

Dr Ian Brooks has written nine books on business management and customer care. Many have been best-sellers. A total of over 50,000 copies have been sold in New Zealand alone. This makes Ian the most published author in business management in New Zealand's history. His most recent books, all published in 2001, are *10 Steps to Becoming Customer Driven*, *The Businessperson's Toolbox of Really Useful Ideas* and *Reality is Crazy: The Sovereign Story*.

A much sought after and internationally recognised business speaker, Ian inspires and entertains over 180 audiences each year in New Zealand, Canada, the United States, Great Britain and Australia. He is one of only six New Zealanders to have spoken at the *Million Dollar Round Table* in America, the world's largest convention of insurance agents.

Ian is one of New Zealand's foremost business advisers. For over 25 years, he has consulted to organisations in New Zealand, Australia, Canada and the South Pacific helping them to survive and grow in this crowded and competitive market place. Ian's clients have included large corporations, such as CSR, Air New Zealand, Telecom, WestpacTrust, Carter Holt Harvey and Fletcher Challenge, and many small and medium-sized businesses. Ian also has experience in the public sector, having consulted to Canada Customs, and a large number of local bodies including the Auckland, Dunedin, Christchurch and Hamilton City Councils. Ian is recognised for his expertise in customer care, organisational change, human resource management, quality management, and business strategy.

You can hear Ian talk about creating customer value and customer relationship management, watch him explain how to turn complaints into cash and see him discuss how to become customer driven, download outlines of his speeches or obtain more information about Ian by visiting **www.ianbrooks.com**

To contact Ian, email ian@ianbrooks.com

Most recent best-sellers

10 Steps To Becoming Customer Driven

The aim in business is to have profitable customers who stay with you for a very long time. This book will show you how to:
- build a customer driven organisation
- so that you can keep your customers longer
- and make more money

$34.95 inc.GST

The Businessperson's Toolbox of Really Useful Business Ideas

Great easy reading, this book is a collection of stimulating articles, bite-sized thought provokers, practical steps and interesting titbits about business and management.

Some of these will make you think, some will make you laugh and some change what you believe. All of them will renew your energy and even inspire you to do things differently.

$39.95 inc. GST

Reality is Crazy
The Story of Sovereign

This is the remarkable story of Sovereign, is one of the most fascinating stories of business in New Zealand's history.

Discover how a company with no name, no staff and no office in 1988 took only 12 years to become New Zealand's largest life insurance company with a market share twice as large as its nearest competitor's.

The Sovereign story is an inspirational tale with important lessons for anyone trying to succeed in business.

$34.95 inc. GST

TO ORDER

For more information about these products
visit: www.nahanni-publishing.com
To order, contact:
Nahanni Publishing Limited
Ph (09) 419 0681 Fax (09) 419 0695
email sales@nahanni-publishing.com

Second To None: Six Strategies for Creating Superior Customer Value
Over 13,000 copies sold in New Zealand!

Business is the art of creating value. In this crowded and competitive market place, those who understand value best will succeed. Those who do not will struggle. This practical and entertaining book will teach you how to be No.1 in your market.

$34.95 inc.GST

Second To None Pocket Edition
Over 17,000 copies sold in New Zealand!

The Pocket Second To None is a useful memory jogger for people who would like a quick reference to Ian's key ideas. It is also a great book to give staff as it explains what your business must do to gain a competitive advantage.

$14.95 inc.GST

Second to None
– Video

Training point.net has taken the essence of Ian's best selling book, *Second to None*, and put it into an easy-to-use five part video series. On each video, Ian shares the secrets of *Second to None*. His easy-going presentations ensure that people everywhere will relate to this vital business message.

$495.00 inc. GST set of 5

Now on Compact Disc
Second To None

Now you can hear Dr. Brooks deliver his internationally acclaimed speech based on his best-selling book *Second To None*. This powerful address will inspire you, teach you and entertain you.

$19.95 inc. GST

The Yellow Brick Road
Over 8,000 copies sold in New Zealand!
The path to building a quality business in New Zealand. A common sense guide to building a successful company. In his usual easy to read and entertaining style, Ian will show you how the principles of quality management can help you to build a profitable business.
$25.95 inc. GST

How to Turn Complaints Into Cash
by Ian Brooks and Michele Comeau
A mini-workbook outlining 5 steps for successfully handling complaints. A must-have for frontline staff and their managers.
$9.95 inc. GST

Getting & Keeping Customers
Powerful techniques for developing customer relations
Customer satisfaction is no longer enough. Customers today are more demanding and more sophisticated. You need to identify your key customers, work to become their partners and turn them into advocates. This mini book shows you how to do it.
$14.95 inc. GST

Complaints are Gifts – *Video*
How To Turn Bad News Into Good News
Ian's straightforward video on handling complaints is vital viewing for everybody. His seven step process for handling the complaining customer will ensure what can be negative becomes a true "gift" to the enlightened organisation.
$295.00 inc. GST

The Brooks Royston Business Report
A twelve-page monthly digest full of stimulating ideas, useful tips and interesting facts to encourage the businessman of tomorrow. You'll read about creating customer value, self improvement, dynamic sales and marketing, small business success and ways to develop staff.
$120.00 inc. GST (12 Issues)